How I Wrote *Jubilee* and Other Essays on Life and Literature

■ ■ ■

How I Wrote *Jubilee* and Other Essays on Life and Literature

Margaret Walker

Edited by Maryemma Graham

The Feminist Press
at The City University of New York
New York

■ ■ ■

The Feminist Press at the City University of New York
The Graduate Center, 365 Fifth Avenue, Suite 5406, New York, NY 10016
www.feministpress.org

First Feminist Press edition, 1990

Library of Congress Cataloging-in-Publication Data

Walker, Margaret, 1915–
    How I wrote Jubilee and other essays on life and literature /
    Margaret Walker; edited by Maryemma Graham
        p.   cm.
    ISBN-10: 1-55861-004-9 (pbk.)
    ISBN-13: 9781558610040 (pbk.)
    1. Walker, Margaret, 1915–   —Biography. 2. Walker, Margaret, 1915–   . Jubilee. 3.
Authors, American—20th century—Biography. 4. Afro-Americans—Intellectual life. 5.
Afro-Americans in literature. I. Graham, Maryemma. II. Title.
PS3545.A517Z47   1989
812'.52—dc20
[B]   89-17017
                                                                                          CIP

This publication is made possible, in part, by a grant from the New York State Council on the Arts.

Cover photo by David Rae Morris
Text design by Paula Martinac

Second reprint

Contents

Preface

When I began graduate school at Northwestern University, I was pleasantly surprised to discover that Margaret Walker was a writer in residence for a quarter. I had read her poetry and the novel *Jubilee*, and I considered myself somewhat familiar with Black literature, having grown up in a traditional segregated community where the art of elocution was still very popular and a major source for the dissemination of works by Black writers, past and present. Walker had made her home in Jackson, Mississippi since the late 1940s and was a faculty member at Jackson State University (then Jackson State College), the largest predominately Black college in Mississippi. Walker belonged to that Black world of the South, her birthplace and nurturing environment, and I, away from that same South for the first time in my life, was frankly ecstatic that I might take classes with such a distinguished foremother, though I did not then know the real meaning of that term nor did I realize the importance and impact of our time there together.

It was less than a decade after the death of Medgar Evers in Mississippi, the integration of "Ole Miss" by James Meredith, and the much less publicized killing of three Black students at Jackson State by National Guardsmen, so Walker brought with her an historical legacy of her own, all of which figured prominently in her brilliant lectures. I remember being constantly amazed at the energy she displayed and the depth and range of her knowledge as she talked only and always of literature. None of us has ever been exposed to Black literature in quite the way that she knew and taught it. There were, no doubt, others like me who had never had a Black teacher outside of a Black school. Everything belonged to her world of literature. Her course was, to put it simply, my first experience in seeing literature and life in relation to one another. I think the most profound lesson that she taught was helping us to see literature as both a creative and scholarly endeavor. She always placed her discussions of literature in the broadest historical and cultural contexts. She so personalized the histories of the authors she spoke about that we all assumed her knowledge to derive from various relationships with these men and women, no matter who they were. Her fondness for intellectual debate was at times frightening; for while she inspired and welcomed it in the classroom and out, every student feared challenging her.

Her two favorite places were the classroom, where she gave her remarkable lectures on Afro-American literature and history, freely sharing personal anecdotes and memories of every black writer whose works we read, and her kitchen, where she talked intermittently while cleaning and cooking fresh collards or preparing her own special version of Louisiana gumbo.

At that time I had little understanding of how Walker or her work was being received. To me she was a master teacher, in the traditional sense of the word, and had a global perspective on literary history, the Black experience, American politics, or any aspect of American life for that matter—that entered her teaching with all the passion that she could muster. I had incorrectly assumed in my naiveté that someone with such a love for language and who thrived on intense intellectual debate would be better represented and viewed in the world of literary criticism. But in point of fact, Walker's remarkable achievement has met with mixed response and somewhat scanty critical attention over the years despite the appearance of her early and best-known volume *For My People*, winner of the Yale Series of Younger Poets Award in 1942, a collection that captured the attention of Stephen Vincent Benet. Some of the reason for this is no doubt due to the fact that Walker has consciously remained far from the center of literary prestige throughout her entire life and yet has continued to produce a highly significant body of poetry, fiction, and prose works. She is widely read—*Jubilee* has been translated into six foreign languages and the U.S. edition has gone through thirty-six printings, having been in print continuously since its publication in 1966. Walker may have been by-passed by the critics, but she is well known to a reading public.

But there seems to be another explanation for the somewhat elusive nature of Walker criticism. Walker is among the generation of men and women who teach and write about Afro-American life and culture with great pride, but whose thinking about American life and culture bear the unmistakable mark of a nascent radicalism, steeled in the Depression years, the heyday of American communism. Walker earned a reputation for her anti-racist, anti-imperialist, antifascist sentiments, which anticipated the emergence of the New Left in the United States and Europe. At the same time, she has an almost purist disdain for the crass materialism and societal disorientation that have become the mark of post-industrial America, remaining firm in her belief in basic human values and the intrinsic worth of man- and womankind. Her works reaffirm the inherent value of work, the importance of family, home, and community. I suspect it is the contradiction between Walker's adherence to certain ideals that are traditionally American and her own social radicalism that makes her critics uncomfortable with her aesthetic vision. As a result, Walker is not included in the standard literary canon and too few students in today's colleges and universities know her name—even as an anthology poet, which she certainly is.

Perhaps it is for this reason more than any other that I am pleased to edit this volume of her essays and speeches. There is no way to ensure that Walker will receive the critical acclaim she rightfully deserves. That will take time and a radical shift in the role and function of literary criticism in our society. What we both hope—Margaret Walker and I—is that this volume will provide a basic introduction to her thought, some sense of her vision as an Afro-American, a woman, and an artist.

Walker's words have much to tell us about literature and life to be sure, but also about a generation of men and women about whom we know so little, people whose visions and persistent efforts made our own lives far more bearable than they might otherwise have been. Often the results of their efforts we celebrate with great fanfare, but seldom do we really know the content of their lives.

My first experiences with Margaret Walker nearly two decades ago naturally returned to me vividly as I prepared these essays. But as I have indicated, it is much more than nostalgia for a lost era that prompted this volume. I have compiled what I consider the most representative selections from more than fifty years of a literary life. What I hope I have presented is a vivid, self-told account of the author's life. When I began to make these selections, I did not realize how difficult my task would be. Like the typical editor of essay collections, I posed the "right" questions to myself. Did I want the collection to be mainly autobiographical? Did I want to focus on those essays that were political, as much of Walker's writing tends to be, or should I favor those essays from which one might deduce Walker's ideas about literary theory and tradition? It did not take me long to realize that such distinctions are not only difficult but almost impossible to make in Walker's case. The activities of Walker's own life, the forces and ideas that have shaped her literary imagination, are inextricably part of and have given shape to the twentieth century as a whole. For this reason, although the six essays in part one, "Growing Out of Shadow" are primarily autobiographical, and the eight essays in part two, "Literary and Other Legacies," are primarily literary criticism, virtually all of the essays contain elements of autobiography, social history, and literary criticism.

Much of the significance of this first comprehensive collection of speeches and essays lies in the fact that they cover the crucial decades between the 1930s and the 1980s, and as such they represent a rare and important legacy. The earliest essay was written in 1943 and the most recent in 1988. Because I wanted this volume to be truly representative of Walker's life and work, I knew I would have to include a number of pieces that were in various stages of completion, many of them prepared as oral texts. Working with these texts meant their substantial transformation—both in terms of content and style—if they were to be useful to the interested reader or the general scholar. In a number of cases, sections were written or rewritten to reflect current knowledge on a subject or to illustrate or document significant points.

My editing, though substantial in some cases, has been to maintain the integrity of Walker's ideas throughout, and to capture the power of her language. I have retained the "period markers" (the generic "he," for example, and "Negro" instead of "Black" in the earlier essays), so that Margaret Walker can be identified as a Black women who sought and achieved her identity in a white, male world that allowed some few Black men access, tolerating no women, let alone Black ones. Finally, I wanted to retain her highly personal and intimate style, which I think is her major link to our present generation.

It is my hope that the reader will find these essays, as I do, a memoir of the nation and of the South, following a path that winds through key literary figures, as well as major social and historical events. For Walker is in every way a witness to and a participant in these events; she is an artist who pursues her own sense of individual identity at the same time she commits herself to the stream of collective history.

In some cases, books are prepared with the assistance of research grants, released time from teaching responsibilities, or funds earmarked for scholarly work. None of these conditions made this book possible. I relied instead on a team of women—my colleagues, students, staff, and friends, who provided support in various ways, and my family, who have never refused any request for childcare assistance.

I am deeply indebted to the women—past and present—of the Afro-American Novel Project at the University of Mississippi—Susanne Dietzel, Barbara A. Hunt, Nadene Dunlap, Lisi Webb-Terrell, and Jennifer Kovach; Sara Selby, manuscript typist in the Department of English; and Ronald W. Bailey, my best critic and comrade. Finally, I must thank Margaret Walker for agreeing that we should do this book and for her confidence in me, and Florence Howe and Joanne O'Hare of The Feminist Press for their support and assistance.

Maryemma Graham

Introduction

Margaret Abigail Walker was born in Birmingham, Alabama, in 1915, into a family of storytellers and musicians, ministers and teachers. The Walker family—three sisters and a brother, parents and maternal grandmother— lived as a closely knit group. Education was strongly stressed, and individual talents were nurtured and encouraged. It was Walker's father who gave her her first writer's journal at age twelve so that she could record her numerous poems and the details of the stories of slavery that were her grandmother's forte. The family moved around during Margaret's childhood, when the Reverend Sigismund Walker accepted posts in various United Methodist churches and schools. Eventually her parents accepted teaching positions in New Orleans where Margaret completed her high school education and began college.

As Walker has reported many times, it was a visit by Langston Hughes to the university where her parents worked that gave her her first opportunity to meet a famous living poet. Not only did Hughes encourage her talent, but he also stressed the importance of formal training, which in his view could only occur outside of the South. A few years later, Walker had her first poems published in *Crisis* magazine.

Walker left for Northwestern University in 1932 to complete her undergraduate education. After graduation, she remained in Chicago to work and write during the middle years of the Depression. Her strong Christian background no doubt made her sympathetic to socialist ideas about social equality and intensified her disdain for all forms of discrimination and exploitation. Like many artists and intellectuals of the 1930s, Walker was familiar with popular Marxist thought and regarded herself as a "fellow traveler," though never a member of the Communist party. Almost always the youngest member of the left front organizations she associated with and often the only black woman participant, she earned an early reputation for her inquisitive nature, her intelligence, and her remarkable talent.

Walker worked three years with the Works Progress Administration (WPA) and became a member of the South Side Writers' Group, initiated by Richard Wright. Both the WPA and the South Side Writers' Group represented two important avenues for advancing Walker's talents. She completed her signature poem "For My People," and developed a close working relationship with Wright that lasted until his departure for New York in 1937.

Walker returned to school in 1939, this time to complete her master's degree at the Iowa Writers Workshop. For My People became a full volume of poems, which she completed to satisfy the degree requirement. After teaching at Livingston College (North Carolina) and West Virginia State College, Walker married Firnist James Alexander and began a family. Walker and her husband moved to Jackson, Mississippi with three children in 1949, where she would teach for twenty-six years at Jackson State College, and become a major cultural force in the community and the college. Securing grants to host symposia, writers conferences, and workshops, Walker established the Institute for the Study of Black Life and Culture, one of the earliest centers devoted to Black studies as an intellectual discipline, and the first of its kind in the South.

In fifty-two years, Walker has published ten books, including For My People (1942), Jubilee (1966), Prophets for a New Day (1970), How I Wrote Jubilee (1972), October Journey (1973), A Poetic Equation: Conversations between Nikki Giovanni and Margaret Walker (1974), For Farish Street (1987), Richard Wright: Daemonic Genius (1988), This Is My Century: New and Collected Poems by Margaret Walker (1989) and the current one, her first collection of essays. An untold number of poems, short stories, essays, reviews, letters, and speeches remain to be collected. When Walker retired from teaching in 1979 at age sixty-four, she did so with the intention of continuing an active career as a writer, public speaker, and community leader. It was at this time that she began the biography of Richard Wright, only to have the book interrupted by illness, a lengthy court battle, the death of her husband, and repeated publication delays.

Since the publication of *Richard Wright*, Walker has been on promotional tours and has returned full time to writing. In addition to forthcoming books (one on Jesse Jackson and a collection of her interviews), she is currently writing a sequel to *Jubilee*, editing a multivolume anthology of Afro-American literature, and working on her autobiography.

This collection of essays and speeches illuminates Walker's importance to the history of ideas that has been reflected in Black writing in America for half a century and to contemporary developments in literary and social thought. In commenting upon the culture of America and the ideas so central to it—religion, family, racial consciousness, the role of women—these essays serve as a useful introduction to Margaret Walker's thought. As much as any individual artist, she reflects the fusion of ideas that she inherited from the radical 1930s, tempered by her own cultural and social background, one that was rooted in a strong religious faith and belief in the ultimate human good. In her essay "Willing to Pay the Price" Walker points out her major concerns as a writer:

> As a Negro I am perforce concerned with all aspects of the struggle for civil rights. . . . Civil rights are part of my frame of reference, since I must of necessity write always about Negro life, segregated or integrated. . . . I believe my role in the struggle is the role of a writer. Everything I have ever written or hope to write is dedicated to that struggle, to our hope of peace and dignity and freedom in the world, not just as Black people, or as Negroes, but as free human beings in a world community. . . . I do not deny, however, the importance of political action and of social revolution. . . . I believe that as a teacher my role is to stimulate my students to think; after that, all I can do is guide them.

Walker's comments bring to mind the works of three early Afro-American women, Ann Plato, Anna Julia Cooper, and Frances Harper.[1] Like Plato, the earliest known Afro-American essayist, Harper, the renowned antislavery poet/activist, and Cooper, a feminist intellectual, Walker pursues her own sense of individual identity while at the same time commiting herself to the stream of collective history. All of these women, along with their texts, have been doomed until recently by what Kenny J. Williams has called the "silence of scholarship,"[2] making it difficult to have a comprehensive understanding of that history. This is particularly true of the essay, a genre that has not been regarded highly among most literary scholars despite its popularity and importance in the history of American literature. Plato and Cooper left only a single collection each and Harper's essays have yet to be collected. Yet they all are overtly concerned with ideas central to American culture and consciousness. All educated and talented, none of these women could be considered radical, yet Cooper and Harper strongly identified with social and political ideas that were far ahead of their times. While Ann Plato's essays reveal little about gender and race, Anna Julia Cooper's *Voice from the South* is a monumental statement on gender oppression. Frances Harper appears to be Walker's closest literary ancestor in her preoccupation with social issues while at the same time maintaining her reputation as a leading poet of her day.

Part one of this book, "Growing Out of Shadow" forms a catalog of comments, reflections, and recollections, drawn mainly from Walker's experience as a southern Black woman who came of age in the second quarter of the twentieth century. "Growing Out of Shadow," the earliest written of the essays (it first appeared in 1943), is a remarkable reminiscence of Walker's childhood in the South. It portrays the mixed emotions of fear and desire and the sense of inevitability that characterized the life of an intelligent person in the early decades of this century. Similarly, "How I Told My Child about Race," written at the beginning of the 1950s, shows the logical development of a racial aesthetic as it confronts the awesome responsibility of motherhood. Walker continues to develop this line of thought as she assumes the role of social critic in "Willing to Pay the Price" and "Black Women in Academia," both of which were written during the social upheavals of the 1960s. The latter essay, unequivocally demonstrating Walker's feminist sentiments, is a forceful critique of the male dominated Black college where Walker spent her entire teaching career, except for an occasional semester as artist in residence at Northwestern. Overworked and underpaid throughout all these years, Walker refused to let this silence her or destroy her creative potential. On the contrary, she fought back, securing grants from public and private funding agencies to host conferences, workshops, festivals, most devoted to literary matters and Black studies.

Each of these essays makes some explicit statement about the working out of the contradictions of race, class, and gender, which is summed up in "Willing to Pay the Price":

> I have faced obstacles and have been forced to run every race with a handicap: I am a Negro born in the United States. All my life I have been poor in the goods of the world. I am a woman. . . . Yet each of these could have been worse. . . . As a woman I have known great personal freedom to do as I pleased and to further my career whether single or married. I have the complete fulfillment of being wife and mother and having a happy home.

If "Growing Out of Shadow" implies coming into consciousness of oneself as a social being, it also implies the development of Walker the artist. And it is in relationship to the latter point that I consider two essays in this part to be hallmarks of the volume.

The first essay was originally delivered as a lecture at the first American sponsored symposium on Richard Wright held at the University of Iowa, Iowa City, in 1971. Walker's "Richard Wright" offers a special perspective on Richard Wright, that of a Black female artist on another Black artist. By the time she was twenty, Walker had received the praise of Langston Hughes and W. E. B. Du Bois as well as Wright. Her poem "For My People" had appeared in the prestigious *Poetry* magazine. She counted Wright among her closest friends during the 1936–39 period and there is no living writer from that period who knew Wright and worked with him as closely as Walker did, no one else who can tell us what she can.

Walker's strengths come through in this essay; she accomplishes the difficult task of subjecting her knowledge of a man she admired and knew well to the careful scrutiny developed over years of literary training and history. Now as Wright is being reassessed by all sectors of the literary community, his reputation carefully guarded by his family and a small circle of his traditional critics, her assessment of the Wright she calls the impulsive, egotistical genius is likely to cause much debate.

When Walker met Wright, she was a college educated, but naive young poet from the South; Wright, a self-educated, Black artist-intellectual also from the South. She had come to Chicago because her parents had listened to Langston Hughes's advice to get her "out of the South." Wright had come, like thousands of Black people before him, to find a better life away from the violence and repression that would have condemned him to a life of eternal hunger, both physical and intellectual. Their mission, therefore, coincided; their talents blossomed in the fertile intellectual and political climate of Chicago.

The second hallmark is the title essay "How I Wrote *Jubilee*." The reconstruction of the thirty-year-long journey to *Jubilee* tells us how this novel's "coming of age" was constantly "robbed" by the responsibilities of a growing family, an unusually difficult teaching job, and perennial forays into public service. This essay makes a contribution to the history of Black writing and to women's writing generally, as much as it demonstrates the meticulousness of Walker's style and the careful attention she paid to the details in recreating the histories and characters of her fiction. Together with Wright's "How Bigger Was Born," this essay becomes a paradigm for the process of artistic representation for Black writers in twentieth-century America.

In part two, "Literary and Other Legacies," Walker brings the skills of the literary critic together with her interest in intellectual history in order to reaffirm the importance of the Afro-American literary heritage. Characters appear in "herstory" in a lively and entertaining way, and Walker's personal portraits of Black male and female writers in "A Literary Legacy" and "The Education of a Seminal Mind, W. E. B. Du Bois," "New Poets of the Forties and the Optimism of the Age," and "Rediscovering Black Women Writers in the Mecca of the New Negro" are graciously rendered. These men and women are her predecessors or contemporaries, and she speaks of them with a primary interest in the ideas that give political, economic, and cultural meaning and continuity to their work as well as her own.

Walker reveals a great deal about Black life and Black literature in these essays, and her easy, biographical and impressionistic style brings to life her sketches of the people she has known. She is enthusiastic about her likes and yet profoundly rational about those things that favor less well with her. In "A Literary Legacy from Dunbar to Baraka," she says of Paul Laurence Dunbar

> He realized that the white world in the United States tolerated his literary genius only because of his jingles in a broken tongue, and they found the old darky tales and speech amusing and within the vein of folklore into which they wished to classify all Negro life. This troubled Dunbar, because he realized that white America was denigrating him as a writer and as a man. . . . The attitude of whites toward Dunbar's poems reflects, instead, another vein of racism. It is a racism that rejects the genius of Dunbar as a poet, and as a man preeminently.

The strokes she paints on her literary critical canvas are broad and precise. She continues,

> Dunbar expressed the language and life of the plantation Negro, whereas Sterling Brown expressed the roustabout, the Black worker, and the strong Black hero in legend and fact. James Weldon Johnson gave us the Black folk preacher, or the sermon tradition, in God's Trombones. Langston has immortalized the modern culture of the city streets, the menials, the domestic servant, the Jesse B. Simples with their homely philosophy, even the so-called bum on the corner, the displaced homeless, demoralized, dispossessed, and denigrated human beings who huddle on the streets of northern cities.

While the impact of a feminist literary consciousness on Walker's thought would need more careful analysis, her comments in "Rediscovering Black Women in the Mecca of the New Negro" are not in any sense ambiguous. There is no new information presented on Alice Dunbar Nelson, Dorothy

West, Georgia Douglas Johnson, Zora Neale Hurston or any of the other half dozen women mentioned in this essay, but what little we know about these women is brought together here for the first time. In addition, the essay suggests that there are social and political issues to be raised, particularly around race and class, as more and more work is done to restore Black women writers to their proper places in literary history.

Two essays in this section, "Some Aspects of the Black Aesthetic," and "The Humanistic Tradition of Afro-American Literature," reflect Walker's views on the important traditions that define Afro-American literature, traditions she herself is part of. What is Afro-American is at the same time Anglo-American and humanistic. These traditions are admittedly dominated by the male voice. That there is no contradiction here is probably due to the fact that though she sees men as forming that tradition, Walker also sees herself and her work as a distinct part of it. Daughter of a music teacher and a minister, Walker inherited an ear for sound, appreciating literature especially in its oral aspect, as part of her enriched cultural environment. Her literary self was generated from her adulation of and identification with literature as a spoken art.

In these essays we are ever mindful of Walker's need to defend the often unspoken values that belie a common Afro-American consciousness and define the chaos and disruption that constantly threaten America. We are ever mindful of the poet in these essays who is constantly searching for ways of giving meaning to her culture through its own formal and structural devices. The essays create a literary landscape that encompasses the past, present, and future. The writing is noticeably passionate, yet thoroughly discriminating. For the reader who has become accustomed to Walker's poetry, the voice in these essays recalls a familiar style and orientation. Like the poetry, these essays are inextricably bound to Walker's own history. Like the poetry too, the essays show a single driving force: a dramatic tension between social activism and artistic imagination. Moreover, Walker, in "The Humanistic Tradition of Afro-American Literature" makes no pretense about assigning a profoundly revolutionary role to art:

> In the twenty-first century perhaps the problem will no longer be that of the color line. There must be a new humanism. A new respect for the quality of all human life must be bred in our young. A new respect for humanity will outlaw war and hate and create new values that do not depend upon money and industry. Some of us are too old and too set in our minds to understand how far-reaching a change of social, mental, and spiritual climate is needed in this country. For some of us this means a whole new world brought on by

violent confrontation and social upheaval, and since we are too old, we are afraid of that. But our children are not too young. They deserve a new mind to face a new universe.

Cultural change like social change depends upon reeducation. Religion, language, communications media, art, music, and literature are cultural instruments that must reeducate all our children with new values for a new century of a new humanism.

Walker's style in this essay is wholly individual; her fondness for verbal rigor, owing much to oracular features and a richly apocalyptic tone, are clearly evident in the conclusion:

> Before we destroy our planet earth, in the words of prophet Isaiah, come now and let us reason together. . . . Humanism is our natural philosophy. Since we are part of history, we are the historical process. . . . Afro-American literature is a reservoir of Black humanism. All America needs to become acquainted with this literature. White America still does not seem to understand that no people can enslave others' bodies and save their own souls. When every human being is holy in the eyes of another, then begins the millennium. Meanwhile, prepare for Armageddon.

The apocalypse is articulated as the Afro-American writer, whether or not he/she confesses to his/her terrible Blackness, becomes the symbolic instrument through which the destruction of one world and the creation of another is accomplished.

No first collection of Walker's essays would be complete without her comments on southern culture, southern literature and William Faulkner of Mississippi, Walker's adopted home state for so many years. Southern literature is defined by geography or cultural context, but Walker explains in "A Brief Introduction to Southern Literature," "The southern writer, like all American writers, but perhaps with more intensity, deals largely with race. He or she cannot escape the ever-present factor of race and the problems of race as they have grown out of the southern society and affected all of America." By defining the South as a multiracial society and its literature an attempt to rise above the racist limitations of any given time or place to present a multiracial and multiclass view of society, Walker departs from many of the popular conceptions of southern literature.

Walker's discussions of Faulkner and southern literature generally highlight another significant point. Despite the abundance of talent emerging from the South, no Black writer has ever achieved recognition by remaining there. Richard Wright is identified with Chicago, New York, and Paris, and certainly not with Mississippi or Tennessee. Ernest Gaines writes about

Louisiana exclusively, but it is California that claims him. The story is the same with modern and contemporary Black writers from Ralph Ellison to Toni Morrison. Thus, in addition to being victimized by the critical neglect that has affected Black writing historically until very recently, Walker seems to have suffered because of her conscious decision to live as a Black woman artist in the twentieth-century South.

As for most of our best writers, for Walker socio-political criteria have always been as important as literary criteria. This is not, however, a pedestrian concern. Walker's preoccupation has led her to explore the internal and external dynamics of the Black experience: to see its manifold cultural products, its philosophical humanism, its militant activism. It is this broader perspective, which always challenges the literary imagination, that has given her critics such difficulty, perhaps, in finding for Walker a "place" in the literary canon.

One thing we might look to these essays to do for us is to help establish what it is that gives Black American literature its distinctive life and voice, why there is a persistence in its mode of expression. For Walker it is that "feeling tone," the abstracted content of the Black experience ever seeking to express itself through the culture's reservoir of verbal landscapes, some spoken, some sung, some preached, some known only through their silence. For Margaret Walker, life and work, as these essays reveal, represent the kind of literary engagement with ideas that should mark its own place in the literary canon and in history.

Maryemma Graham

Notes

1. See "Introduction" in the following edited collections: *Essays; Including Biographies and Miscellaneous Pieces, in Prose and Poetry, Ann Plato; A Voice from the South, Anna Julia Cooper;* and *Frances Ellen Watkins Harper, Collected Poems* (New York: Oxford University Press, 1988 for all editions).

2. Kenny J. Williams, "Introduction," *Essays; Including Biographies and Miscellaneous Pieces, in Prose and Poetry, Ann Plato* (New York: Oxford University Press, 1988), p. xxxvi.

Margaret Walker, c. 1942; photo: New York Public Library

Part One:
Growing Out
of Shadow

Growing Out
of Shadow

When I was five, I was busy discovering my world, and it was a place of happiness and delight. Then, one day, a white child shouted in my ears "nigger" as if he were saying "cur," and I was startled. I had never heard the word before, and I went home and asked what it meant, and my parents looked apprehensively at each other as if to say, "It's come." Clumsily, without adding hurt to the smart I was already suffering, they sought to explain, but they were unable to destroy my pain. I could not understand my overwhelming sense of shame, as if I had been guilty of some unknown crime. I did not know why I was suffering, what brought this vague uneasiness, this clutching for understanding.

When I went to school, I read the history books that glorify the white race and describe the Negro either as a clown and a fool or a beast capable of very hard work in excessive heat. I discovered the background of chattel slavery behind this madness of race prejudice. Once we were slaves and now we are not, and the South remains angry. But when I went home to the good books and the wonderful music and the gentle, intelligent parents, I could see no reason for prejudice on the basis of a previous condition of servitude.

I went to church and I wondered why God let this thing continue. Why were there segregated churches and segregated hospitals and cemeteries and schools? Why must I ride behind a Jim Crow sign? Why did a full-grown

This essay was first published in *Common Ground*, 4, no. 1 (1943): 42–6.

colored man sit meekly behind a Jim Crow sign and do nothing about it? What could he do? Then I decided perhaps God was on the side of the white people because after all God was white. The world was white, and I was Black.

Then I began to daydream: It will not always be this way. Someday, just as chattel slavery ended, this injustice will also end; this internal suffering will cease; this ache inside for understanding will exist no longer. Someday, I said, when I am fully grown, I will understand, and I will be able to do something about it. I will write books that will prove the history texts were distorted. I will write books about colored people who have colored faces, books that will not make me ashamed when I read them.

But always I was seeking for the real answer, not the daydream. Always I wanted to know. I lay awake at night pondering in my heart, "Why? Why? Why?"

I heard Roland Hayes and Marian Anderson sing, and James Weldon Johnson and Langston Hughes read poetry. In the audiences were well-dressed, well-behaved colored people. They were intelligent, yet they were not allowed to sit beside white people at concerts and recitals. Why? Every night Negro cooks and maids and chauffeurs and nursemaids returned home from the white people's houses where their employers were not afraid to sit beside them.

I learned of race pride and consciousness and the contribution of the Negro to American culture. Still I was bewildered. America was a place of strange contradictions. The white grocery man at the corner who was so friendly when I was in his store thought it a crime for a white and a colored boxer to fight in the ring together. But he did not think it a crime for a Negro to be drafted to fight for America.

I decided vaguely that the white man must think these things because of fear; because he felt insecure. Perhaps he was a little afraid of what would happen in a free America. How did I first discover the color of my skin? I had only to look in my mirror every morning to know. I must say it appeared to me a good healthy color. But there is a difference in knowing you are Black and in understanding what it means to be Black in America. Before I was ten I knew what it was to step off the sidewalk to let a white man pass; otherwise he might knock me off. I had had a sound thrashing by white boys while Negro men looked on helplessly. I was accustomed to riding in the Jim Crow streetcars with the Negro section marked off by iron bars that could not be moved. For a year and a half I went to school in a one-room wooden shack. One year when my father's schoolwork took him out of town constantly, my mother lived in fear of our lives because there was no man in the house to protect us against the possibility of some attack. Once, we climbed the fire escape to see a movie, because there was no Negro entrance, and after that we saw no movies. Another time my mother stood for hours upstairs in a darkened theatre to hear a recital by Rachmaninoff, because there were no seats for colored. My father was chased home one night at the point of a gun by a drunken policeman who resented seeing a fountain pen in a "nigger's" pocket. My grandmother told the story of a woman tarred and feathered in the neighborhood. A mob came and took her from her home because it was rumored that a white man was visiting her. Although they took her deep into the woods, her screams were heard by relatives and neighbors. My grandmother heard them, too. Next day the woman's family went to the woods and brought her home. She was still alive, so they removed the tar and feathers with turpentine. She was horribly burned and scarred.

And always the answer and the question in a child's mind to each of these was "Why? Why do they do these things?"

Negroes congregating on a city block to argue and talk about the race question imitated what they heard from the pulpits or what the white folks told them: "The trouble with the Negro problem in America is just we needs to git together . . . We don't co-operate . . . We always kicking one another . . . This is a white man's country and Black man ain't got no place in it . . . We just cursed by God, sons of Ham, hewers of wood and drawers of water . . . Our leaders are crooked and they betray us . . . We need to get a little money and make ourselves independent of the white man . . . If it wasn't for the white man we'd be way back in the jungles of Africa somewhere . . . We oughta thank the white man for bringing us to this country and making us civilized . . . Trouble is we scared to fight, scared to stick up for our rights . . . We'll fight for the white man but we won't fight for ourselves . . . All the progress we've made we owe to the white man . . . I hates a white man worsener I hates poison, left to me I'd kill up every paleface in the world . . . Don't let 'em fool you when they grinning in your face, they want something . . . Only God can help us . . . It takes time, that's all, to solve the Negro problem . . . All we got to do is humble ourselves and do right and we'll win out . . . Colored man hurts hisself most of the time . . . All we got to do is do like the children of Israel and the slaves done way back yonder, pray . . . Colored people oughta get out of the notion that they are Negroes . . . That word *Negroes* is what hurts us. . . ."

But all of it was no real answer to the anxious questioning of a child burdened constantly with the wonder of what race prejudice is.

When I went away to college in my teens, I left the South with mingled emotions. I had been told that Negroes in the North were better off than Negroes down South; they had more sense and more opportunities; they could go any place, enjoy recreational facilities such as parks and movies, eat in restaurants without discrimination; there were no Jim Crow transportation restrictions, and if Negroes were subjected to any indignity, they could sue the person or company involved; there was no such thing as lynching. Best of all, Negroes could vote.

I was, nevertheless, shy and afraid over the prospect of going to a white school; I might prove backward as a result of my southern training. I had also perforce become somewhat antiwhite myself and I feared coming into close contact with white people. Yet I anticipated a new kind of freedom once I crossed the Mason-Dixon Line.

Imagine my great hurt to discover that few of the wonderful promises came true. I was refused service in restaurants in Evanston and Chicago time and time again. In the South I had suffered no similar embarrassment because there I had known what to expect. I discovered that most of the Negroes in the northern colleges and universities were from the South, for the majority of Negroes in the Middle West had no money with which to take advantage of higher education.

What was most amazing was my discovery of my own prejudices and my first realization of the economic problem.

Because of the nature of segregated life in America many Negroes have misconceptions of white life. I was no exception. As servants, Negroes know certain elements of white life and characterize the whole in this way. My first step toward understanding what it means to be Black in America was understanding the economics of the United States.

In the South I had always thought that, naturally, white people had more money than colored people. Poor white trash signified for me the lazy scum of the marginal fringe of society with no excuse for poverty. Now I discovered there were poor white working people exploited by rich white people. I learned that all Jews were not rich. I discovered that all Negroes were not even in the same economic class. While there were no Negro multi-millionaires, there were many wealthy Negroes who made money by exploiting poor Negroes, who had some of the same attitudes toward them that rich whites had toward poor whites and that prejudiced whites have toward all Negroes. Imagine my amazement to hear a white girl tell me she was forced to leave Northwestern because she had no money. But I, a poor Negro girl, had stayed even when I had no money. They never threatened me with expulsion. Yet I did not find a white school in the Middle West free of prejudice. All around me was prejudice. To understand the issues out of which it grew became my life's preoccupation.

A year out of college found me working with poor whites—Jew and Gentile—and poor Negroes, too. In Chicago, for the first time I began to see that Negroes, as almost entirely a working-class people, belong with organized labor. My background was so thoroughly petty-bourgeois, with parents who belonged to a professional small-salaried class, that I had not understood that people who worked with their brains were also workers. I knew we were poor and decent, and that was all I knew. In the South, many, if not most, petty-bourgeois Negroes are antiunion, antistrike, and antiwhite. This, of course, is not strange when one considers the history of Negroes in unions in the South, their forced role as scabs, the brutal treatment they received as such, prior to the Congress of Industrial Organizations (CIO), the general nature of Negro life in the South, threatened always by sinister undertones of white violence.

Thus there began for me in Chicago a period in which I learned about class in the United States. As soon as I began working in close contact with whites, I discovered startling things peculiar to both racial groups, all adding up to one main conclusion: that whites suffer psychologically from the problem of race prejudice as much as Negroes. I began to see race prejudice as a definite tool to keep people divided and economically helpless: Negroes hating whites and whites hating Blacks, with conditions of both groups pitiful, both economically and psychologically. I saw, too, that it was not beyond the ability of both groups to reach understanding and to live peaceably side by side, that the organization of Negroes and whites by labor was certainly one step forward toward that end.

The second step toward understanding what it means to be Black in America came in understanding the political problem. By 1932 and 1936, Negroes had, out of the dire necessity of destitution, become politically conscious even in the Deep South, where they had no real voice in politics. In the North, the East, and particularly the Middle West, the Negro vote assumed significant proportions and in many instances proved effective in the balance of power.

In 1936 I cast my first vote in Chicago in a Presidential election. It was a great time to come of age. There had been four years of the New Deal, and many of the ills and evils of our society, as they immediately touched Negroes and all poor people, had been somewhat alleviated. We had benefited from the Works Progress Administration (WPA), the National Youth

Administration (NYA), the Federal Housing and Federal Farm Administration, Social Security, the WPA adult education program; we had benefited in many instances where there had previously been evil practices of discrimination. I began to dig into the historical background of politics in America, to read the record where Negroes were concerned. I began to see parallels. When the thirteen colonies revolted, they revolted on the premise that taxation without representation is tyranny. Yet that is precisely what the Negro suffered in the South still. Moreover, poor white people as well had no voice in their government. If the truth were nationally known and understood, the small number of votes cast in electing southern representatives and senators to Congress, as compared with the population, would not merely appear ridiculous but alarming. Not that these citizens of America were too indifferent to vote; they were disfranchised under the pretense of a poll tax not paid or a grandfather clause. The old saying that a voteless people is a helpless people became a basic fact in my understanding of the Negro problem.

A third step came from a growing world perspective. As a child, reading the history books in the South, I was humiliated by some unhappy picture or reference to a Negro. Such items made me burn all over. It was as if we were cut off from humanity, without sensitivity. I could make no connection between my life became self-supporting, yet I had not connected myself with working women all over the world, with poor peasant women who are white as well as Black. Now I began to reach out. I saw it was eternally to the credit of Negroes in America that we were represented in Spain on the side of the Loyalists with soldiers, nurses, volunteer workers, our humble gift of an ambulance, our moral support. We can be proud that Ethiopia found a willing ear for help from us. While white America is far too prone to appreciate the struggle of people in distant lands and forget the problems on its own doorstep, its disadvantaged groups are often too obsessed with their own problems to see further than the bridge of their nose. I realized it was essential for Negroes to be identified with every heroic struggle of an oppressed people, with the brave Chinese, the Indians, the South Africans, the Negroes in the West Indies who fight for liberty. Now that we are engaged in a global war, it is even more essential that all peoples of the earth gain a world perspective and become conscious of our common humanity and man's struggle to be free.

Yet I am sure that economic, political, and social understanding is not all. There is need for a new type of spiritual understanding, and I use the word not in its narrow religious meaning. I am concerned with something far more meaningful in the lives of individual men and women, of greater practical value and far better potentialities for personal and social growth. Once the human spirit is washed clean of prejudices, once the basic needs of people are considered, and not the pocketbooks of the few nor the power of a handful; once institutionalized religion is liberated into religious meaning, of necessity there must begin to bloom upon the earth something spiritually more durable than any of the mystic conceptions of religion that humankind has thus far brought forth. Then no person will look at another with fear, patronage, condescension, hatred, or disparagement, under pain of one's own spiritual death.

How I Told My Child about Race

A little over two years ago, at Easter time, our children received an album of records of nursery songs recorded by Frank Luther. Among the thirty-seven songs is a group of lullabies. These songs have become household bywords. The two older children quickly memorized each one. The baby, less than two years old, is already cutting his musical teeth on one of these songs.

Among the lullabies is one particularly concerned with race. It is introduced in this fashion: "Do you know there are babies all over the world? Nice brown ones and pink ones and Black ones and cute little yellow babies. Their mothers love them and sing to them just as your mother does, all over the world. Now here is what a Chinese mother sings to her little yellow baby to put him to sleep:

Snail, snail, come out and be fed
Put out your horns and then your head
And your papa and your mama
Will give you Boy Martin.

I believe this was our children's first introduction to the subject of race. Before they grew old enough to ask the questions that inevitably face all Negroes who are parents and who live in America, we were trying to

This essay was first published in *Negro Digest* (August 1951), pp. 42–6.

introduce them painlessly to a world of love and not hatred, of tolerance and not prejudice.

But there is no way to live without pain and sooner or later we have had to face the problem. I do not know whether we have faced it as honestly and courageously as we should, but there came the day when Marion asked, "Mama, are we colored?" and I said, "Yes." Imagine how I froze inside when she came to tell me how someone she loved and admired in our own race had called her the hated word.

"Mama, she called us a bad name!"

"What did she say?"

"She called us niggers! She said, 'All right now, you niggers get out of here.' Are we niggers?"

I said, "No, you are Negroes, but not niggers." And with that came the sneering retort: "What are they then? They are not white, so they must be niggers."

This did not come from the white world. We have fought hard to protect them from any hostile attack upon their delicate and sensitive natures— avoiding the segregated bus for trips to town, carefully ignoring their requests for water from the Jim Crowed fountains in department stores and other public places; telling them they would not enjoy the pictures in the forbidden theatres or the exciting rides in the "white only" parks—but suddenly we faced the insensitive facts of life among our own.

Sooner than we hope, we must stand up and face the issues honestly. Once the damage is done, there is no way we can erase the emotional hurt, but we can strive to appeal to their growing understanding in an effort to buttress them with truth as well as love. We have their curiosity to satisfy as well as their feelings to consider.

Living as we do, deep in Dixie, facing every day not merely the question of race but the problems of Jim Crow or segregation, we have a tendency to build an unreal world of fantasy, to draw a charmed circle around us and within this circle to feel safe; to close our eyes to the bitter struggle, and to forget if possible all the ugliness of a world as near as our front door and closer than the house across the street. We live on a college campus and here in a completely Black world we often feel a kind of escape. We build a tower in which we rationalize our way of life. These become our protective coloring: the poker face, the masked eyes held straight ahead, the deaf ears, and the silent tongue.

Our children, however, do not allow us to remain cowards, complacent, or withdrawn. They force us to face the bitterness and dare us to explain the pain. Much as it hurts, we owe them the truth.

There was the evening when we took a relative to the railway station and discovered that a chain prevented the Negroes from ascending the stairs to the Jim Crow train until the whites had all moved ahead. This had not happened to us before that night. I saw the bewildered look on Marion's face and the signs of nervousness gathering in James's eyes. Quickly I sought to explain that those people must walk farther to board the southbound train than we, and so they went first; in the morning we walk farther for the northbound train and we move ahead first. I do not think the children were convinced. They sensed something strange about the division of the people into two groups and this I did not discuss. I shall never forget the shock and puzzled look on their faces.

Children discuss race among themselves as much as their elders. They make their own rationalizations, and pin their own half-truths upon the web of lies that surrounds them. Marion and her playmates have had such a discussion. This past year she went to school as a first-grade pupil. At school she saw newsreels of the war in Korea as well as life on the domestic front at home in the United States. She came home bubbling with the excitement of any growing child slowly discovering a world constantly full of wonder. One day after school:

> "Mama, guess what so and so said?"
> "What did she say?"
> "She said she would like to be white."
> "Would you?"
> "No."
> "Why not?"
> "Because white people try to destroy colored people."

Then I knew it was time to stop for a long-needed talk, not merely about race and color but in order to instill the kind of pride in race and in one's self that was part of my upbringing and of which I have never been ashamed. It was also time to stop the beginnings of prejudice against white people that we as Negroes acquire unconsciously and that I believe is just as egregious as that imposed against us. I told Marion that not all white people are bad, that every person is born with the capacity of loving as well as hating and that those who hate without a cause are blind and ignorant and do not understand why nor what they are hating. I told her that as long as people hate each other there will be wars such as we have now in Korea and that people must be taught to love just as they are taught to hate before the world can be what we want it to be. Then she asked me this:

"If a colored woman married a white man, what would their baby be, and would that be all right?"

I confess this set me back on my heels. I looked at my husband and he was grinning. My bottom lip must have dropped, because Alex kept egging me on: "Go on. Tell her. Do you believe in mixing the races?" I struggled to rise above evasion. This is what I told her: "If a colored woman married a white man their baby would be considered colored no matter how white the baby's skin would be. There are a lot of people in the world who think it would be all right, and there are a lot of people who think it would be all wrong. It depends on the people. They probably won't ever agree unless maybe someday anybody can marry whomever they choose without fear of what people will think or say or do, because perhaps by that time race hatred will be forgotten."

Insofar as pride in race is concerned, I began to question my child as a result of her questioning. I sought to know if she, only a few short weeks before her seventh birthday, thought of famous Negroes in terms of race and with pride. I knew she had heard boxing matches over the radio, featuring Joe Louis and Ezzard Charles, only a few nights ago Marian Anderson on the Telephone Hour, a Sunday baseball game broadcast with Jackie Robinson playing for the Brooklyn Dodgers, and I have read poems to her from *The Dream Keeper* by Langston Hughes, so I was not surprised when I asked her for names of famous people and she named these. What did surprise me, however, was to hear her name George Washington, Abraham Lincoln, and Alexander Graham Bell in the same breath, and coupled with these names. She did not distinguish people according to race and she did not know which of these was colored and which was white. Her father and I were pleased. We want her to be proud that she is a Negro, yes, but we also want her to think in terms of people as people and not only of race. We want her to think kindly of all people without malice, without bitterness, without hatred, and without prejudice.

So I have told my child about race, and in so doing I faced the same problem as that of answering such questions as Where do babies come from? How was I born? Where is God?, and Why can't I see him?

Just as I had to tell Marion that babies live inside their mothers until they are large enough to be born and live alone. That God is all the Goodness in the world that is all around us but that we cannot see Him because He is a Spirit without face or hands or eyes or feet.

Even so I had to tell her that she is a Negro who can be proud that she is one of millions of colored people in the world and that she is a member of the human race.

Willing to Pay the Price

Here in the United States "Success" with a capital "S" is measured in materialistic terms of fame and fortune. An artist is not basically concerned with this kind of success. A creative worker dealing with the fiery lightning of imagination is interested in artistic accomplishment, and I have spent my life seeking this kind of fulfillment. As long as I live, this will be my quest; and, as such, the superficial trappings of success can have no real meaning for me. I do not really care what snide remarks my confreres make nor how searing the words of caustic critics are. Life is too short for me to concern myself with anything but the work I must do before my day is done.

If there are any single factors that have blessed my life with the best, they are intelligent parents who not only fired my ambition and demanded that I set my sights high and be judged by standards of excellence, but also insisted that I seek spiritual values and crave righteousness and integrity more than money; remarkable teachers in three of the nation's finest academic institutions; and lessons learned from bitter experience and from fellow writers. Linked with these factors has also been an indispensable element of luck and good fortune.

True, I have faced obstacles and have been forced to run every race with a handicap: I am a Negro born in the United States. All my life I have been poor in the goods of the world. I am a woman. And since birth I have been dogged with ill health. Yet things could have been worse. Despite these handicaps and race prejudice in America, which I discovered early and have lived with all my life, I was able to complete my education, attending, while doing so, some of the nation's finest institutions. Yes, my lot might have been worse; I have often heard poor whites speak of their lack of opportunity to get such an education. As a woman, I have known great personal freedom to do as I pleased and to further my career whether single or married. I have the complete fulfillment of being wife and mother and having a happy home.

Despite poverty and ill health, my needs have always been met in the nick of time. Once in a Chicago slum I was startled while riding on the elevated train and looking over the very neighborhood where I lived to hear a woman say, "I wonder how in the world people live there!" Often it was difficult for me to obtain the twenty-five-cent fare to ride the elevated train to Evanston and classes at Northwestern during my senior year, but I managed somehow, and with the help of my wonderful teachers made A's just the same. Other Negro students often did not speak to me because they were embarrassed about the way I looked—wearing dresses and coats that had seen better days and ragged stockings. When I was working on the WPA (Works Progress Administration) Writers' Project, my sister and I lived on eighty-five dollars a month, but we got along because the cost of living was not high. We paid five dollars a week for a room with kitchen privileges, and mostly we cooked and ate at home. Ten dollars' worth of groceries provided staples for two weeks. A favorite meal was a can of mushroom soup, a can of corn kernels, and four wieners. On paydays we splurged on steak or oysters. I still think nothing tastes as good as porterhouse steak tasted then in Chicago. But there were days when we did not have a nickel for a White Castle hamburger, and I can remember feeling faint with the smell of food cooking, and going home to sleep off my hunger. Friends often fed us, and always did so on holidays. Yet those days in Chicago give me some of the most wonderful memories of my life.

About that time a renaissance was developing in the arts: painting, acting, music, and writing. Studio parties were held in smoke-filled rooms, with much intellectual or political conversation going on; and although I never learned to drink the beer, the food was wonderful—cold cuts and rye bread and lots of pickles. On the Project many writers were struggling, some of whom were destined to become famous; among these were Willard Mottley, Richard Wright, Frank Yerby, Nelson Algren, Arna Bontemps, and

Jack Conroy. This Writers' Project turned out to be one of the best writers' schools I ever attended. It was Nelson Algren who asked me the question, "What do you want for your people?" That query motivated me to finish my poem "For My People." Later, Nelson reviewed the book *For My People* when it was published. Wright and I met my first year out of college. We became fast friends and corresponded for two years after he went to New York. While I was writing poetry, he was writing the novellas in *Uncle Tom's Children*, and *Native Son*. I am sure that this friendship made an indelible impression on my writing career. Marxism was the intellectual fad then, and those who were not Stalinists were Trotskyites. It was the time of the Memorial Day Massacre and the beginning of the CIO; Roosevelt was our hero, the man of our age, as youngsters in the sixties considered John F. Kennedy. Bravely, I sought to repudiate my academic background, for in this crowd it was no recommendation.

Pride in my folk heritage as a Negro was, however, very much the rage. Race pride was something I was taught as a child. My father went to Tuskegee for a few brief months in the days of Booker T. Washington, but he found what he wanted in Atlanta in the days of W. E. B. Du Bois. My mother had heard as a girl the words of Kelly Miller and Roscoe Conklin Simmons. She read poems by Paul Laurence Dunbar to us along with John Greenleaf Whittier's "Snow-Bound." I can never remember when *The Crisis* and *Opportunity* magazines were not in our house, along with the Methodist Church papers like the *Christian Advocate*, and such Negro newspapers as the *Chicago Defender*, the *Pittsburgh Courier*, and the *Louisiana Weekly*.

Later, after moving to New Orleans, we attended as many cultural programs as possible. Thus, long before my hegira to Northwestern I heard Marian Anderson, Langston Hughes, James Weldon Johnson, and Zora Neale Hurston, and saw the play *Green Pastures*. Throughout my high school days I made a scrapbook of famous Negro Americans, whether they were athletes, politicians, or blues singers. At school there were my mother's spring musicals and recitals and the memorable times when she accompanied a visiting artist who sang or played the violin. On Sunday afternoons in the chapel, with its rich patina of wood wainscotting, I listened to wonderful music, looked out at the sun setting, and wondered if ever there would be such a golden moment again. In Chicago, during the late thirties, my sister Mercedes and I had such moments: in Grant Park, during the summer concerts under the stars; at Orchestra Hall, hearing Mercedes play with the symphony orchestra; and at Northwestern University, hearing Harriet Monroe or Carl Sandburg read poetry.

When I was a little girl and some lady asked me what I wanted to be when I grew up, my father answered for me, "Tell her you are going to be an elocutionist!" Most people don't talk about elocution these days, and I smile now to remember the puzzled look on many people's faces when I responded to my father's suggestion. My parents were convinced early that I would become a public speaker, and I was standing before audiences by the time I was five.

I cannot remember when I learned to read; my mother taught me by the time I was four, and I in turn read the comic strips and *Tales of Uncle Wiggly* to my younger sisters. I loved books, and by the time I was eight I knew I wanted to learn to write books. My father had many volumes in his library, and I grew up believing that with the exception of human personality nothing in the world could be finer than a good book. The hope that I could become a poet seemed impossible at first, for I was laboring under the general illusion that the poet has some special mystique beyond the knowledge of ordinary human beings. In my adolescence I lost that illusion, for I wrote poetry or some kind of jingle almost every day. Earlier, when I was ten, I became enamored with the story of my greatgrandmother's life, as told to me by my grandmother and as recorded in *Jubilee*, so that I nurtured the secret hope that I would learn to write prose—fiction and nonfiction—as well as poetry, in free verse and traditional forms. My education and much of my environment accordingly were geared to that purpose. My parents taught school. My sisters, my brother, and I teach school. We are teachers in spite of ourselves and despite any other ambition we may have had. Yet we teach different things. One sister teaches little children because that is what she has always wanted to do. My brother teaches mathematics and social sciences in a high school despite his fervid interest in progressive jazz, and I teach college English because I had decided that if I ever taught school it would be on the college level.

My father must have gotten his ideas of education from the philosopher Alfred North Whitehead, for he followed a definite theory about our education. I never was good in arithmetic, algebra, or any form of mathematics, but I loved literature and history and I concentrated on those subjects. Once in college, I thought I might switch my major to the social sciences, particularly sociology, but my father said, "No, you cannot swap horses in the middle of the stream." He strictly forbade my taking any courses in philosophy because he insisted that in my teens I was not mature enough and, besides, I lacked the logical mind. So I have learned philosophy, both idealistic and materialistic, by reading the major works of great philosophers since I left college. My father had a tendency to choose courses for all of us, and we never went wrong if we followed his advice. He also insisted that we study foreign languages early, so I had studied four languages before I was twenty. He was convinced that once a person was mature it was a mistake to try to learn a new language.

Father also believed that my writing poetry was only a puberty urge. My mother did not agree and neither did I. When I was eighteen and had completed my junior year in college, I asked him if he still thought my writing was only a puberty urge. He laughed and said, "No, I guess not; you will probably continue writing for the rest of your days." It was my father who first bought me a permanent notebook for my poems and told me to keep them together. He was a scholar, as fine as any teacher I have ever known in three great universities. He won every prize available in college and seminary for English, Greek, Latin, and Hebrew, and took his M.A. degree from Northwestern in Biblical Literature. I realize that his ambitions for me were very great despite the fact that I had disappointed him by not being a boy. Had I been a boy, he would have made a preacher out of me, but since I wasn't a boy he decided to make the most of it. It was his desire that I have a Ph.D. in English before I became twenty-one, but luckily for me, neither health nor finances would permit it. Once out of college I went to work on the Writers' Project, and I was twenty-five the summer I received my M.A. degree. My father did not live to see me get this degree, but I know he would have been happy about it. He did live to enjoy *For My People*.

Early in my life my parents instilled certain principles and beliefs in all their children, and these principles remain thoroughly ingrained in all of us. First, they provided us with a deeply religious background. For them, the Protestant ethic was Puritan to the core, a stern moralistic code of duty and responsibility, and prayer was a daily occurrence in our home. We grew up in Sunday School and church, and I was amazed when I went away from home to discover that everybody did not go to church. We were taught that we were expected to achieve and that the achievement must be one of excellence. However, we were taught not to expect excessive praise for a job well done. Even on the day my parents received a copy of *For My People*, my mother wrote a prim little note saying, "You have made us very proud." And that was that.

I do not believe in giving advice, since most people don't want it, and I am loath to set myself up as an authority on any subject, but I can pass along some of the things told to me and some of the things that I have learned from other writers:

1. Write what you know about, not about something of which you know little or nothing.

2. Work hard and revise and never be weary of trying to achieve perfection. Above all, try never to print anything of which you may be ashamed in the future.

3. Never pay to have your work published.

4. Study the masters and learn from them. Read the great writers and imitate them.

5. Become your most severe critic. Don't be easily satisfied and know when you have done the best you possibly can.

Writing poetry is not, as many people think, something that strikes one as a bolt from the blue. It is a skill that must be developed as a result of patient practice, hard work, and study. Every spare moment of my early years was devoted to learning and developing this skill. In those years I benefited greatly from the advice and encouragement of teachers whom I shall never forget. I was also inspired and helped by a number of writers and poets whom I was fortunate enough to know, and who left an indelible impression on me. I was sixteen years old when I had the first opportunity to talk directly with a living poet, Langston Hughes, who read some of my verses one night and encouraged me to continue writing. In Chicago, during my WPA days, I met the writers George Hill Dillon and Peter DeVries. George Dillon helped and encouraged me and suggested that I read all the French symbolists. As a result, I read Baudelaire, Rimbaud, Verlaine, and Mallarmé.

I never met a writer with more drive than Richard Wright. Even though he was an intellectual giant of his time, talented to the point of genius, it was his drive that compelled him to achieve. In the workshop at Iowa University I had the firming-up that I needed to become a professional writer. All of those days were not easy, but they were very profitable. At Iowa I began writing to Stephen Vincent Benét, and I have a small handful of letters in which he gave me good advice about writing poems, particularly ballads. Naturally I prize these letters, along with those of Richard Wright and Langston Hughes, that mark those early years.

From these random notes I think my philosophy of life should be clear. I believe anybody can achieve regardless of handicaps—if he is willing to pay the price. Some people are born to achieve, but writers, while born talented, must work hard to develop their talents. It has always been my thesis that writing grows out of living, and not living out of writing, so that living comes first. I realize, however, that writing for many is a reason for existence.

My raison d'etre is to express life as I see it. Everything in life comes with a price. Hard work is a foregone conclusion. Some of us as Negroes were born in slums, uneducated, mistreated, and deprived, but we have achieved in spite of this. I have always heard it said that writing is a difficult and lonely business. I would not say that I have been exactly lonely, but I do know that any writer worth his salt has had to work hard. One thing I always wanted to avoid was becoming a dilettante. I have always wanted to be a serious, full-time writer. I have been instead a full-time teacher, and nobody really writes effectively while teaching full time. Therefore, in one sense all my books are not written, and I am in that sense a failure, since I never sacrificed anything for writing. Rather, I sacrificed writing to have a family, to keep a job, to make a living. The best writers have given up everything for the sake of their art, and therein lies part of their success. Now as I face retirement from teaching, I look forward to full-time writing. It is a lifelong dream, but who knows whether it will ever come true? Perhaps I am now too late. Have I really put first things first?

I am not one who believes that my writing and my being a Negro are related purely by accident of birth. All I have ever written or desire to write is motivated by the fact that I am a Negro living in America, one of a minority group unrecognized or rejected by the dominant group. We Negroes are America's stepchildren, as Langston Hughes has so beautifully said, and we have a need to express our feelings of being rejected, of being oppressed, of being denied, and of being brutalized and dehumanized. Being a Negro in America is my central theme, with the concomitant problems of being a Negro woman, being exploited and scorned, being hated and despised. The meaning of my life is tied up irrevocably and inextricably with this theme.

All my life I have longed to see the signs go down—the signs of segregation, of degradation, and discrimination. Even as a child I wondered if I would live long enough to see this happen. For I never doubted that it would; I just wondered how long it would take, and if I would live to see the day. Now I have lived to see the signs go down, the signs I sat behind on street cars and buses, the curtains I rode behind on trains, ropes I stood behind in theaters and restaurants. In bewilderment and pain I grew up looking at the signs, and now, thank God, most of the signs are down.

I never shall forget hearing Judge Hastie say in 1952 in Jackson, Mississippi, when someone questioned whether men's hearts and minds could be changed by laws, "We are going to make segregation illegal, against the law, and then we will proceed from there." The Supreme Court and the Congress of the United States have declared segregation illegal and unconstitutional. Yet we also know that men's minds and hearts have not entirely changed. We cannot be satisfied, for school integration is still only tokenism and threatens to remain thus as long as residential segregation prevails; but we know that the start has been made.

The Negro revolution of the 1960s came like a breath of fresh air blowing through the United States, but it was only a light breeze, not a storm. The fundamental facts of segregation still remain. I think all of us must have held our breath when the Reverend Martin Luther King began his noble adventure in Montgomery. But when Martin Luther King went to Birmingham, I think the whole nation knew we were on our way.

We became increasingly proud of the later "sit-ins," "wade-ins," "stand-ins," and the like. All of these events, however, did not complete the change in men's hearts and minds. The earlier murders of Emmett Till and Mack Charles Parker and other shootings and attacks were followed by still other heinous crimes. The tragic death of Medgar Evers saddened us all. He was our neighbor and friend, as well as a brave young leader of the Negro people in Mississippi. As an intrepid young fighter against discrimination and segregation he gave his life, but he did not die in vain. His death shocked the world and aroused the conscience of this nation. His death and the deaths of others give us hope that there will be a better nation and a better community because they died.

As a Negro, I am perforce concerned with all aspects of the struggle for civil rights. As a writer, however, my commitment has to be to the one thing I can do best, and that is to the business of writing. Richard Wright used to say that nothing should come before a writer's art but his writing. Civil rights are part of my frame of reference, since I must of necessity write always about Negro life, segregated or integrated. In the twenty-first century, perhaps, there will be no need for this view, but I belong to the twentieth century, and there are a few things left on the agenda, a few pieces of unfinished business where the Negro is concerned in America before this century ends.

I believe firmly in the goodness of the future, and that in the final analysis right will prevail—not through goodness and optimism, necessarily, but through stress and travail. I believe that man's destiny is a spiritual destiny and that God is not merely transcendent but also immanent, deeply involved in the affairs of men since men are made in His image, each with a spark of the divine and a human personality always maintaining that divine potential. Sometimes in America the future of the Negro looks hopelessly dark, but against all evil this divinity and the human spirit, or human personality, will shine like a light.

Am I a gradualist, an activist, a segregationist member of the Black Establishment, or where do I stand? I do not believe any Negro in good conscience can acquiesce in the vicious evil of segregation, but I also believe that not everyone is brave enough to die—yet everyone has his role. I believe my role in the struggle is the role of a writer. Everything I have ever written or hope to write is dedicated to that struggle, to our hope of peace and dignity and freedom in the world, not just as Black people, or as Negroes, but as free human beings in a world community.

I know segregation has seemed to benefit some Negroes who have battened upon the oppressed, but these are not in the majority. I am a firm believer in the value of education in this struggle. It is what my great-grandparents believed. What I have in mind is not necessarily formal education. I have seen many intelligent and educated people who never went to school; however, I believe it is important to cultivate the intellect. Our schools and colleges should not strive merely to turn out graduates as we turn out goods from factories.

Perhaps I do not understand fully the meaning of the slogan "Black Power." Sometimes I think I do and then again I wonder. Richard Wright's book *Black Power* concerned the emerging nations of Africa and social ferment in Asia. "Black Power" as a slogan for Negro Americans is something else.

On one issue I am clear. I do not believe that hating any man solves the problem of race or any other problem. The failures of a capitalist society in the final stages of high financial imperialism need not be imitated by the victims of such a materialistic system. I firmly believe that hatred, like anger, works on the physical glandular system as well as on the moral fiber of our nation, and in doing so, can bring no positive good. Although I do not believe in servility, I do not believe that we should insult our friends or say we do not need them because they are white. Perhaps our genuine friends will overlook our bad manners, but I wonder if our children will do so and not imitate our precept and example?

What the white man has done to us through centuries of oppression is patently clear. He has brutalized and stigmatized us, and tried to dehumanize us, but we, like Job, have nevertheless maintained our own integrity. The mechanistic system itself makes for dehumanization, impersonality, and depersonalization, but the system also is doomed to change as all things change.

The Negro has a great spiritual role to play in America. He has already evidenced that role in his folk contribution to the literature, music, and religious life of America. Negroes helped to build America, and a full knowledge of Negro history reveals that all American life has been influenced by them. The Negro does have a special mystique, and it has not come from hatred. In the deep welter of Negro emotion, suffering, and pride, we have a profound spirituality to offer the United States on the road to the fulfillment of her great destiny. If she refuses and turns away, we cannot use that as an excuse for our not offering this precious and rare gift.

I do not deny, however, the importance of political action and of social revolution. I know that the thinker is slow to act and that fact may damn him; but I also know that before action can implement thought, there must first be an idea. I believe that as a teacher my role is to stimulate my students to think; after that, all I can do is guide them. In a century since freedom, our great job as Black people has been to develop intellectuals who could lead us and who, in turn, could transform ideas into action. This, I believe, is the way, the truth, and the life.

If western civilization steadily declines and the twenty-first century finds the balance of power to lie in Asia and Africa, the destiny of Negro Americans will nevertheless be bound up with the destiny of the United States. White America may very well be ending western civilization as the nonwhite people in the world ride a high road to destiny. But unless Negroes quit these enslaved shores, we are still Americans, unrecognized though we may be. Perhaps there is hope that our Black cities, like our Black art and Black pride and Black suffering, will change the political course of the United States and alter the social system so that justice and brotherhood may prevail before it is too late. I am not sure we can depend on that. White people ask southern Negroes daily, "Don't you think race relations are better? Don't your people feel that they have made progress?" In Mississippi, where I am now, these are hard questions in the face of all the violence we have seen. Just as in Montgomery, Birmingham, and Selma, Alabama; New Orleans and Plaquemine, Louisiana; Memphis and Clinton, Tennessee; Little Rock, Arkansas; and Albany, Georgia—we have many problems still in Grenada, Natchez, Jackson, and McComb, Mississippi.

Segregation has been outlawed and made illegal, and the United States government no longer gives legal sanction to Jim Crow, but all the people's hearts have not changed. The violent, ignorant, rabid, and unjust are still among us. Whether they will gain political and economic control and thus continue to poison our lives as well as their own is an open question. Whether the people of good will who have been afraid to speak out or stand up and be counted on pain of economic pressure, political reprisal, or violent death will come forward now and assert their strength is another question. But we Negroes know that the United States stands at the crossroads of western civilization and that we Black people are truly the test of democracy. We are the conscience and the soul of America. Either we must all perish together or we must all learn to live together, and white citizens essentially must make this decision. Scientists tell us that in this new space age man has his self-destruction already in his own hands. Perhaps we are on the verge of annihilation, and the grasping materialistic economy behind the hypocrisy of spiritual idealism will go down in ashes to defeat.

But if we are not on this verge, and if America can weather the Negro revolution and successfully meet the test of genuine American democracy, then the twenty-first century will usher in the millennium with social justice, international understanding, and peace for all members of the human race.

Black Women in
Academia

The first woman in my family to experience discrimination in academia was
my mother. She was the first woman in her family to get a college degree and
to teach school. Her father and uncle taught school, but her mother did not
get an education. My mother was the youngest of seven children and her
older sisters, like her mother, had done washing and ironing and cooking for
white folks. They wanted my mother, a talented musician, to have an
opportunity to get an education and to be a lady. So they sent her from
Pensacola, Florida, to Washington, D.C., to boarding school. Although she
received a scholarship to Howard University for her college training she did
not accept it. She was homesick for Florida. After three years scrubbing
floors to help pay for her schooling, she wanted nothing so much as to go
home.

Completing high school, she returned to Pensacola, where she met my
father and became engaged to be married. That next school term she taught
country school in Greenville, Alabama, making only a few dollars a month.
The first year she lived with her grandmother, and the next September she
married my father and went to Birmingham, Alabama, to live.

Six weeks after I was born she was asked to teach music in the small

This essay is adapted from a speech given at an annual meeting of the National
Association of Black Behavioral Scientists, in Atlanta in 1972.

Methodist church school, Central Alabama Institute, which was located close to the church my father pastored in Mason City. After a brief year at Central, my father was moved to a church in Marion, Alabama. In the middle of the year my mother received a letter asking her to return to Central Alabama Institute. She wrote she would very much like that, but she had to stay with her husband, and added that she could only accept the work if they offered my father a job as well. They hired my father and thus began twenty years of teaching in church schools for my mother and father. In all that time my mother's salary never was as much as a hundred dollars a month.

My mother finished college in New Orleans by going to school at night for four years while working in the day. Obviously this would not have been possible had not my grandmother lived with us and done all the cooking, washing, ironing, and house cleaning. When my father received his master's degree at Northwestern, after going six summers, my mother was offered a scholarship to complete her graduate work in music but could not accept because of her children and family. I was a teenager, and she said it was the wrong time for her to leave me as well as my sisters and brother. Her teaching job grew so impossible that she suddenly quit while I was in the middle of college. The day I graduated from college my father also ended his teaching career and went back to the ministry as a pastor. My mother said she worked around the clock teaching private pupils, music classes, conducting the singing, playing the organ, conducting the orchestra, arranging music, and traveling with the singing male group, all for a pittance plus harassment. She had no rank or tenure and she was reduced to receiving a few dollars (about thirty-five) in a small bank envelope. This was during the Depression. Soon afterward she began working on the WPA, where she made more than she had teaching.

I also graduated to the WPA, but unlike my mother, I had gone uninterrupted through Northwestern, getting my degree in English when I was nineteen. After three years I went to graduate school in order to get a master's degree and teach. Getting my master's in one school year nearly killed me. I was on NYA (National Youth Association, a government supported agency) and had so little money I ate lunch only once a week when a friend bought it. When I went home in August, my father lifted me from the train and I was in a state of collapse. For eighteen months I was unable to work.

Meanwhile, one of my sisters had graduated from music college and had taken a job teaching music at a small school in Mississippi. Her salary was forty dollars a month, and like my mother, she worked seven days a week. This included playing for vespers and church on Sunday and leading the choir practices. She said the only time she had for herself was at night from close to midnight until dawn. After teaching two years in Mississippi, she went to Knoxville, Tennessee, for a larger salary but the same back-breaking schedule. Then she taught at Tuskegee; after two years she went back to Chicago to get her master's degree, then moved to Paducah, Kentucky. Throughout these eight years her salary remained less than two hundred dollars per month.

In disgust she left the South, saying she would never teach in a Black college again, that she could not take the humiliations heaped upon her by the college administration while nearly killing herself with work and making so little money. She went to New York City and plunged herself into the concert field, only to discover that the hardest thing in the world for a Black woman to do is make a living playing on the classical concert stage. After several grueling years of playing with a symphony orchestra, town hall recitals, on radio and television, and touring the South and Midwest, she gave up and went into the public schools of New York City, where at least the pay was good, although the work was neither stimulating nor rewarding.

My second younger sister, meanwhile, had graduated from college and was substituting in the public schools of New Orleans. For many years no woman teacher was allowed to marry, and many women kept their marriage a secret. Until she retired, she taught in the same school where she began teaching during World War II. She, too, went summers to graduate school, taking her master's degree in child psychology from the University of Chicago. For fifteen years she served on every curriculum committee for primary instruction established by the Board of Education, New Orleans Parish. In the late fifties she took a sabbatical and went to Columbia to study for a year, taking primary supervision and curriculum building. She has suffered a triple discrimination. In addition to being Black and female, she was an early victim of polio, and for a long time there was a question about whether she could be appointed to teach. It so happened at that time that Franklin Delano Roosevelt was President, and we argued if the President of the United States could be president in a wheel chair, surely she could teach. She neither uses a crutch nor a cane and never has been in a wheel chair. Just the same she has endured much with constant reminders that she is handicapped. Some years ago she went back to school and received another master's degree from Loyola University, with special emphasis on teaching mathematics and science to elementary school children. She drives her car and is rated as an excellent teacher. And, although she has no wish to be a principal, she has thrice been denied the job of primary supervisor.

As for myself, my teaching career has been fraught with conflict, insults, humiliations, and disappointments. In every case where I have attempted to make a creative contribution and succeeded, I have immediately been replaced by a man. I began teaching thirty years ago at Livingstone College in Salisbury, North Carolina, for the handsome sum of one hundred and thirty dollars a month. I was very happy to get it. I had a master's degree but no teaching experience. I arrived in Salisbury at two-thirty one cold February morning, and although I was expected, there was no one at the station to meet me. I finally found a taxi to take me to the campus, and banged on the door of the girls' dormitory for fully a half an hour before anyone opened it. Less than three hours after I went to bed, the matron ordered me out for breakfast at six o'clock and told me I had an eight o'clock class. My life was arranged for me hour after hour and controlled by a half-dozen people. I was resented in the town and by some faculty and staff people because I was replacing one of their favorite people. (And I didn't know this person from Adam's cat.) I had absolutely no social life and spent most of my afternoons and evenings in my room writing. That summer I had to move out of the dormitory into a private home and then back again to the dormitory in the fall. I won the Yale Award for Younger Poets that summer and began getting job offers from everywhere. I felt strong pressure to stay at Livingstone, but when I went home, my parents had accepted a job for me at West Virginia State College. It paid the grand sum of two hundred dollars a month and my dear mother felt it was her duty to grab it before somebody else did. Meanwhile at Livingstone, I went to my first College Language Association[1] (CLA) meeting at Hampton Institute. As I observed then, men were completely in control of the CLA, and only recently did the organization get a woman president.

At West Virginia State College I never had a stable living situation. The night I arrived I had no place to go. The dean had leaned out of his bedroom window to tell the driver to take me to so-and-so's house for the time being. The next day they moved me to another place where I was clearly unwanted. I slept there but had to get up cold mornings and walk through the snow to the dining hall. After Christmas I moved into an apartment I expected to share with another young woman, and found myself in a threesome. That didn't work, and again my dear mother solved it by arriving and putting all my stuff outdoors. Next I moved in with a crazy woman. Finally the administration let me go where I had been told all year I could not stay, to a dormitory. Five places in one school year. I had had it! Had I been a man, no one would have dared move me around like that.

When the National Concert and Artists Corporation offered me a contract to lecture and read poetry for the next five years, guaranteeing me three times as much as my nine months salary at West Virginia, I took it. I had suffered constant embarrassments from my immediate supervisor, who declared that it looked as if I were the head of the department instead of an instructor. "All you can hear is Margaret Walker!" she said disapprovingly. I would arrive in my classroom to be told by my students that the head of the department had begged them to leave because I was late. They replied they would wait because they learned more from me in fifteen minutes than they learned from some people in an hour. That did not help my situation. I was hissed at when I arrived at the chairman's office and was told he was too busy to see me. When I insisted, I was told, "I thought you were a student," as if that was the way to talk to a dog much less a student. But the real harrowing experience of my life came at Jackson State College. In September 1949, when I began teaching in Jackson, Mississippi, I was married and the mother of three children. My youngest was nine weeks old the day I began. For nine months everything went well and members of the administration kept saying they were honored to have me, until I moved my family and furniture. They saw that my husband was sick and disabled from the war, that I had three children under six years of age, that I was poor and had to work, I was no longer their honored poet, but a defenseless Black woman to be harassed.

That summer the president openly attacked me in a faculty meeting by accusing me of talking about the low standards of education in Mississippi. He told me in so many words that if I didn't like what went on in Mississippi I could find myself another job. He ranted and raved so, I was close to tears, and a neighbor nudged me and said, "Let's go home, Mrs. Alexander." Had I been single, I would have quit that day, but I had three children and a husband, and I had just moved. So I bowed my head and decided to stay on. Perhaps I should have taken another job. That faculty meeting put me on ice for a year. Almost nobody darkened my door except my housekeeper and my family. A year later, I was ordered to produce a literary festival for the seventy-fifth anniversary of the college and was told to write some occasional poetry and write and produce a pageant for the occasion. I said then that if I succeeded I would have to leave here, and if I failed, I would also have to leave. I succeeded through much stress and strain and public embarrassment, and then by the hardest effort, I secured a Ford Fellowship and left. I stayed away for fifteen months, and when I returned to a substantial raise, I also had another child.

From 1954 until 1960, at Jackson State in Mississippi, my salary remained well under $6,000 each year. Meanwhile I had devised a humanities program to suit the needs of Black students in Mississippi. We not only raised the cultural level seventy-five percent, but among other things, we also provided a unit on race in the modern world and the great contributions of Black people to the modern world. Trouble over the humanities program nearly drove me out of my mind. I was replaced by a man who openly said he was hired to get rid of me. Words cannot express the hell that man put me through with consent of the administration. Finally the administration decided it had enough evidence against me to fire me from the college, at a time when my husband was recuperating in the hospital from his third operation and could not work any longer at the job he had been doing for seven years. I was called into the president's office, and in the presence of the dean, I was vilified and castigated and told that if I would just resign, everybody would be happy. Knowing it had already been announced that I was going to be fired, I replied, "Why should I resign a job that I have done well every day for thirteen years and that I like? You fire me!" The president changed the subject. I knew I was entitled not only to tenure but also to an appeal and that my contract said I could not be fired except for moral turpitude and insubordination. I stood up and insisted that he tell me one thing: "Gentlemen, do I understand that I am fired?"

"Now Mrs. Alexander, you know we have not said anything about firing you."

"I just wanted to know."

The dean said, "I knew it would end like this. I knew this would be it."

I said, "Well, you know, we live till we die, don't we? Regardless, we live till we die."

Then began the death struggle for me to return to graduate school. I contended that I was no longer willing to be classified as the equivalent of the Ph.D. because I was a poet. My salary was not equivalent, and so I was determined to go back and get that degree that everybody worshipped so much and that brought more salary to the holder. My children were growing up and getting ready for college. My husband was disabled, and I absolutely needed the money. I was tired of living on borrowed money from one month to the next.

I had difficulty getting another appointment with the president. Finally he consented to see me. I told him I felt insecure, and I was worried about my future. I needed more money and I felt the best way to ensure a raise was to go back to graduate school. He informed me that I wasn't going to get any more money. I was doing well enough. I had a house and a car, and he was sure I was doing better than I ever had done in my life. Besides, he said, you are too old to go back to school and you have been so sick you are not even a good risk for a loan. I got into my car and went out to the edge of the town. I got out where nobody could see or hear me, and I screamed at the top of my voice. Then I went back to plan my strategy.

I borrowed five hundred dollars from the credit union and got another three hundred from the college as salary, plus additional money from my husband. I took my two younger children, ages six and eleven, and I went back to the University of Iowa to summer school. There I inquired about my chances of returning for the doctorate degree, of using my civil war novel for my dissertation, and of getting financial assistance.

I went back to Jackson State College for another hellish year, but in September 1962, I managed to get away. I put pressure on the administration and I managed to get half of my salary for two years, while I taught freshman English at Iowa for the other half. I signed a note to borrow my salary for the third year. My mother kept my children. Had she not been living, I could not have gone back to graduate school. (I had two children in college during those three years. One graduated a week before I did.)

When I returned to Jackson with my degree, I asked not to be involved with humanities. Instead, I tried to formulate a new Freshman English program modeled on the Iowa Rhetoric Program for writing themes with a relevant reading list. After a year the college administration did not so much as give me the courtesy of saying they would not require my services in that capacity the next year. They simply replaced me with a man: not a man with superior training, rank, or ability, just a man.

I turned again to my interest in creative writing, which I had first started at the college, and taught courses in literary criticism, the Bible as literature, and Black literature. After another so-so year, I devised a Black studies program that was funded under Title III. My years with that program were the happiest of my teaching career at Jackson State College. As I told the late dean, I had worked for over twenty years at Jackson State, and, although it may have been profitable enough to meet my bills for the barest necessities, it had not been pleasant for a single day.

Note

1. The College Language Association is the primary organization of Black language and literature professionals, founded during the days when the Modern Language Association and the National Council of Teachers of English did not encourage Black membership or participation.

Richard Wright

I first saw Richard Wright on Sunday afternoon, February 16, 1936, in Chicago at the Old Armory Building, where he was presiding over the Writers' Section of the First National Negro Congress. I last saw him on the evening of June 9, 1939, in New York City, where I had gone to attend the League of American Writers' convention, see the New York World's Fair, and, I hoped, to sell my novel, *Goose Island*. During those three years, I think we were rather good friends. Looking back upon that relationship, it seems a rare and once-in-a-lifetime association which I am sure was not merely of mutual benefit but rather uncommon in its completely literary nature. And by "literary" I do not mean "arty" or pretentious or any form of dilettantism, which he despised. I believe now that we shared a genuine interest in writing, in books, and literature. Moreover, we were mutually engaged in those three years in a number of associations and undertakings that, given the perspective of thirty-five years since their inception, seem uncanny in their significance.

We were writers together on the Federal Writers' Project of the Works Progress Administration (WPA) in Chicago; we were members of the South

Reprinted with slight alterations from *Richard Wright: Impressions and Perspectives*, edited by David Ray and Robert M. Farnsworth (1973), by permission of University of Missouri. This essay originally appeared in *New Letters* 38, no. 2 (Winter 1971): 182–202.

Side Writers' Group; we were interested in the little magazine, *New Challenge*; we had mutual friends and associates who were also writers; and during those three years we were struggling to publish for the first time in national magazines and books. We had varying and unequal degrees of success, but both of our talents found shape during those years. I know I owe much to his influence and interest in my writing and publishing poetry at that time: I am not so sure how much he owed to me. One thing I do know, however, is that during this three-year period Richard Wright wrote "Almos' a Man," *Lawd Today*, "The Ethics of Living Jim Crow," "Blueprint for Negro Writers," all the five stories in *Uncle Tom's Children*, and *Native Son*. Prior to our friendship, although he had published poetry in leftwing magazines, he had not published one significant piece of imaginative prose. I had the privilege of watching the birth of each of these works and seeing them through various stages of conception, organization, and realization. His first scissors-and-paste job was the first I had ever witnessed, and I rejoiced with him as each of these works found publication.

Langston Hughes originally introduced us (and when Wright died in Paris, Langston wrote me from London the news of their last visit). Wright in turn had introduced me to Arna Bontemps and Sterling Brown, who were on the WPA. In our South Side Writers' Group were Theodore Ward, the playwright, and Frank Marshall Davis, the poet, who was working for the Associated Negro Press. On the Project were such writers as Nelson Algren, whose sole work at that time was *Somebody in Boots*, Jacob Scher, James Phelan, Sam Ross, John T. Frederick, Katherine Dunham, Willard Motley, Frank Yerby, and Fenton Johnson.

Wright and I went to some of the same studio parties, read the same books, spent long evenings talking together, and often walked from the North Side, where the Project was located, on Erie Street, downtown to the public library, or rode the El to the South Side, where we lived. He gave me books for presents: an autographed manuscript of "Almos' a Man," a carbon copy of *Lawd Today*, which I had typed gratis; a copy of Flaubert's *Madame Bovary*, of e. e. cummings's *The Enormous Room*, and an autographed copy of *Uncle Tom's Children*. For two years after he went to New York we corresponded, and for the most part I kept his letters. My gifts were invariably of food and wine and cigarettes, and perhaps, what he valued most, an exchange of ideas, moral support, and a steadfast encouragement, because I had no doubt from the beginning that he would win fame and fortune. When I met him, his apprentice years were over, and in that last year of his ten Chicago years, it was easy to see where he was headed.

I

Going back in my memory to that Sunday afternoon in February 1936 when I saw Wright for the first time, I remember that I went to the meeting because I heard it announced that Langston Hughes would be there. I met Langston first in New Orleans on his tour of the South in February 1932, when he appeared in a lecture recital, reading his poetry at the college, New Orleans University, where my parents taught. He encouraged me then to continue writing poetry and he also urged my parents to get me out of the Deep South. Four years later to the very month, I wanted him to read what I had written in those four years. Six months earlier I had graduated from college at Northwestern and I still had no job. I was anxious to stay in Chicago, where I hoped to meet other writers, learn something more about writing, and perhaps publish some of my poetry. I tried to press my manuscripts on Langston, but when I admitted I had no copies, he would not take them. Instead, he turned to Wright, who was standing nearby, listening to the conversation and smiling at my desperation. Langston said, "If you people really get a group together, don't forget to include this girl." Wright promised that he would remember.

A month passed and I heard nothing. I presumed he had either forgotten or he hadn't gotten a group together. Meanwhile, on Friday, March 13, 1936, I received my notice in the mail to report to the WPA Writers' Project directed by Louis Wirth and located downtown in the Loop on Wells Street. Six weeks later I received a penny postcard inviting me to the first meeting of the South Side Writers' Group. Twice I left the house and turned back, the first time out of great self-consciousness because I felt I looked abominable. I had nothing to wear to make a nice appearance and I was going to the far South Side where I felt those people would make fun of me. But my great desire to meet writers and end my long isolation conquered this superficial fear. I made myself go. Once at the address given on the card, I discovered I was very late. I thought the meeting was over and I heard people laughing as I blurted out, "Is this the right place or am I too late?" I heard a man expounding on the sad state of Negro writing at that point, in the thirties, and he was punctuating his remarks with pungent epithets. I drew back in Sunday school horror, totally shocked by his strong speech, but I steeled myself to hear him out. The man was Richard Wright. Subsequently, as each person present was asked to bring something to read next time, most people refused. When I was asked, I said, rather defiantly, that I would. I left the meeting alone.

Next time, when we met at Lincoln Center on Oakwood Boulevard, I read a group of my poems. I was surprised to see they did not cut me down. Ted Ward and Dick Wright were kind in their praise. I remember Russell Marshall and Edward Bland were also there. Bland was killed in the Battle of the Bulge. I was completely amazed to hear Wright read a piece of prose he was working on. Even after I went home I kept thinking, "My God, how that man can write!" After the meeting Wright said he was going my way. He asked me if I were on the Writers' Project, and I said yes. Then he said, "I think I'm going to get on that Project." I looked at him in complete disbelief. I knew it took weeks and months to qualify for WPA plus additional red tape to get on one of the professional or art projects. What I did not know was that he had already been on WPA for some time. He was merely transferring from the Theatre Project to the Writers' Project.

The next week when I went to the Project office for my semiweekly assignment, Wright was the first person I saw when I got off the elevator. He quickly came over and led me to his desk. He was a supervisor and I was a junior writer. My salary was $85 per month while his was $125. He hastened to explain that he was responsible for his mother, his aunt, and his younger brother, and he was, therefore, the head of a family though single, while I had only my sister as my responsibility. A year later I advanced to $94, but then he was getting ready to leave Chicago. Gradually a pattern established itself in our relationship on the Project. I went downtown twice weekly with my assignments on the *Illinois Guide Book*, and afterward I spent most of the day in conversation with Wright. Sometimes I was there at the end of the day, but I never worked daily, as he did, in the office. I worked at home and went looking for news stories, or covered art exhibits and made reports. And that is how I came to have a creative assignment after I had been on the Project about nine months. Wright, on the contrary, worked with the editorial group and sandwiched his writing in between when there was a lull in office work. He had taught himself to type by the hunt-and-peck method and I was astounded to watch him type away with two or three fingers while his eyes concentrated on the keyboard.

The first writers' conference I attended was a Midwest writers' conference early in the spring of 1936, shortly after I met Wright. He was speaking and asked me to attend. Afterwards, in our South Side Writers' Group meeting, I was recalling the incident, and Frank Marshall Davis asked me if that wasn't a Communist group. I was confused and said, "I don't know." Then I looked at Wright, who only grinned gleefully and said, "Don't look at me!" The whole thing sank in gradually that he was a Communist. I honestly didn't know what communism or Marxism meant. I had had no courses in sociology, economics, nor political science while I was a student in college. I majored in English, with emphasis on the European Renaissance, and except for a few basic and general courses in mathematics, science, psychology, and religion, I concentrated on literature, history, and languages. My sister knew more about Hitler and Stalin than I did. I was even more puzzled when Jack Scher tried to give me some advice one afternoon, leaving the Project. He said, "Margaret, I hope you will get to know all these people on the Project without getting to be a part of them and all they represent. You are young and you have talent. You can go far, so observe them but don't join them." Only years later did I begin to understand him. I thought he was seriously talking about the labor movement which was so exciting at that time. The CIO (Congress of Industrial Organizations) was just being organized, and I heard John L. Lewis speak several times. The AF of L (American Federation of Labor) had never wanted Negroes in their trade unions. Wright seemed intensely interested in the labor struggle as well as all the problems of race and what he explained to me was a "class struggle."

One of the first books he handed me to read was John Reed's *Ten Days That Shook the World*. I was fascinated. That same summer Maxim Gorky died and I had never before heard the name. I read quickly his *Lower Depths* and *Mother* and then I read the so-called "Red" Archbishop of Canterbury's book, *The Soviet Power*. Having very little money to spend on books, I bought them as I bought my clothes, on layaway, and under the influence and partial tutelage of Wright, I put five Modern Library Giant books in layaway: Karl Marx's *Das Kapital*, Evelyn Strachey's *The Coming Struggle for Power*, *The Complete Philosophy of Nietzsche*, Adam Smith's *The Wealth of Nations*, and a novel by Romain Rolland. A whole year later and long after Wright was in New York, the books were mine. One afternoon Wright quoted from T. S. Eliot:

Let us go then, you and I,
When the evening is spread out against the sky
Like a patient etherised upon a table;

And he exclaimed, "What an image!" Something exploded in my head and I went home to find my copy of Louis Untermeyer's anthology, *Modern American Poetry*, and reread Eliot. I remember how dull he had seemed at Northwestern, when the teacher was reading aloud, and even when I heard Eliot reading on a bad recording, "We are the hollow men . . ."

I began James Joyce with *Portrait of the Artist as a Young Man*; then read *Ulysses*. Wright used James Joyce as an example when he was writing *Lawd*

Today, being struck by a book that kept all the action limited to one day, but he considered *Lawd Today*, which I retyped for him, as one of his worst works. I think it was actually his first completed novel. I remember that he regarded Melanchtha in Gertrude Stein's *Three Lives* as the first serious study of a Negro girl by a white American writer.

Stephen Crane's *Red Badge of Courage* I knew, but not *Maggie, A Girl of the Streets*, which was Wright's favorite. I think from the beginning we differed about Hemingway and Faulkner. Although I had read some Hemingway, I had not read much of Faulkner, and despite Wright's ecstatic feeling about *Sanctuary*, I found it revolting, possibly because I was still strongly influenced by a moralistic and puritanical background.

I never worshipped at the altars of either Hemingway or Faulkner, but Wright deeply admired both. I read James Farrell's *Studs Lonigan* at Wright's request, but I could not work up a passion for Clifford Odets's *Waiting for Lefty*, which the WPA Theatre Project had produced while Wright was working for the Theatre Project in Chicago, as well as Erskine Caldwell's *Kneel to the Rising Sun*. Caldwell's *Tobacco Road* was a nationally famous play and a Pulitzer Prize winner, as was Paul Green's *In Abraham's Bosom*, which I particularly liked. John Dos Passos's *The Big Money* and Carl Sandburg's *The People, Yes* were current favorites that we both loved. Reading Marcel Proust was an experience I associate completely with Wright. Wright's favorite D. H. Lawrence was *Sons and Lovers* rather than *Lady Chatterly's Lover*: I confess now that my understanding of *Sons and Lovers* was much better when I was much older, best of all after I became the mother of sons. But I am sure all this must have led to some discussions we had then of Sigmund Freud, Carl Jung, and Felix Adler, especially of Freud. Also it is very important to remember when we read the later Richard Wright, in a book like *The Outsider*, written after his association with Sartre, that way back there in the thirties he was intensely interested in Nietzsche, Schopenhauer, and above all, the novelist Dostoyevski. Wright and I differed keenly on our taste and interest in the Russian writers. He believed that Dostoyevski was the greatest novelist who had ever lived and the *Brothers Karamazov* his greatest novel. I never felt quite that extravagantly about him, even though I plunged into the book at that period for the first time. Turgenev and Conrad were two others on whom we differed. I had read some of both and now I found a renewed interest, but I have never felt as sympathetic toward Joseph Conrad as Wright did. I liked the element of adventure in Conrad's sea tales such as *Typhoon*, but I have never liked the short fiction; I realize now that I have deeply resented what I feel is ersatz in

Conrad's treatment of Africa and the Negro. The two works Wright and I discussed most were *Lord Jim* and *The Nigger of the "Narcissus."*

If there were two literary books that were Wright's bible they were Henry James's *Collected Prefaces* and *The Art of the Novel* and Joseph Warren Beach's *Twentieth Century Novel.* It must have been Henry James who first interested him in the long short story or the short novel, which he correctly called by the Italian name, the novella. When we consider, however, that Wright was also familiar with the short fiction of Dostoyevski, Flaubert, Melville, D. H. Lawrence, James Joyce, and Thomas Mann as well as James, one cannot be too certain who first led him in this direction. I know, however, that he had been interested in the short story form for a long time. I vaguely remember and realize now that he loved Edgar Allan Poe, A. Conan Doyle, and Jack London, and that he talked of having read pulps, detective stories, and murder mysteries long before his serious reading began with Mencken while he lived in Memphis. He was tremendously impressed with Mencken and I never read his essay on "Puritanism in American Literature" without thinking of Wright.

Suspended in time somewhere between the Writers' Project and the South Side Writers' Group, possibly in the parlor of the house where I lived, three forms of writing took place in our consciousness, conversation, and actions. We sat together and worked on the forms of my poetry, the free verse things, and came up with my long line or strophic form, punctuated by a short line. I remember particularly the poem, "People of Unrest," which Wright and I revised together, emphasizing the verbs:

> Stare from your pillow into the sun
> See the disk of light in shadows.
> Watch day growing tall
> Cry with a loud voice after the sun.
> Take his yellow arms and wrap them round your life.
> Be glad to be washed in the sun.
> Be glad to see.
> People of Unrest and sorrow
> Stare from your pillow into the sun.

Likewise we sat together and worked on revisions of "Almos' a Man" and *Lawd Today.* We discussed the difficulties of Negro dialect, and Wright decided he would leave off all apostrophes and the usual markings for sight dialect. We discussed folk materials and the coincidence of our interest in Negro spirituals and the work songs and what Wright called the dozens (cf. the opening lines of "Big Boy Leaves Home"). I remember both of us were working on a piece using the words of the spiritual "Down by the Riverside." "Silt" was a forerunner of the long short story "Down by the Riverside," which Wright wrote that same year. I felt hopeless about my novel manuscript, which became *Jubilee* and of which I had three hundred pages in first draft written at that time. We both decided I should put it away until another time.

I was pleasantly surprised to learn, early in January of 1937, that I would be granted a creative writing assignment and my novel chapters could now be turned in as my work assignments. The day I was told, Wright was absent from work and I learned he was at home ill with a bad cold. When I went home that afternoon, my sister and I decided to buy some oranges and take them to him. Then I could tell him my wonderful good news. We found him in the house on Indiana Avenue, in bed in a room that I could not understand, because it had one door and no windows. Imagine my shock when I later realized it was a closet. He was very happy to hear about my good luck and both of us were embarrassed about the oranges.

One cold windy day in Chicago, walking downtown from Erie Street, Wright and I crossed Wacker Drive, turning our backs to the wind, and went into the Public Library at Washington and Michigan Avenue. I was returning a pile of books, and Richard said he felt tempted to teach me how to steal but he would resist such corruption. I assured him that I felt no compulsion to steal books.

II

Wright left Chicago for New York on May 28, 1937. It was Friday afternoon and payday on the Project. We generally went to the same checkcashing place nearby, and when we were standing in line for checks Wright was behind me, so he asked me to wait for him. About that time one of the silly, young gushing girls on the Project (as Nelson Algren used to say, "Dames who don't know the day of the week") came up to me, and she said, "Margaret, tell Dick he's got to kiss all us girls good-bye." I laughed at her and told her, "Tell him yourself, I wouldn't dare!" When I got my check, I looked around and sure enough all the young white chicks were mobbing him with loving farewells—so I left. Outside on the street, I had walked a block when I heard him yelling and hailing me. I turned and waited. "I thought I told you to wait for me?" he said, grinning impishly. I said, "Well, you were very busy kissing all the girls good-bye. I'm in a hurry. The currency exchange will close." We cashed the checks and got on the El. Fortunately the car was not crowded and we got seats on one of the long benches. He said, "When I go tonight, I will have forty dollars in my pocket."

"Oh, you are leaving tonight?"

"Yes, I've got a ride and lucky for me. It's a good thing 'cause I surely can't afford the railroad fare."

"Well, you'll make it."

"I hope I can get on the Writers' Project there. I've got to find work right away, and I hope I'm not making a mistake, going this way."

"How can you say such a thing? Aren't you on your way to fame and fortune? You can't be making a mistake."

"I knew you would say that. I guess you won't think again about coming to New York too, and soon."

"No, I've got to help my sister. I can't leave now."

"I think together we could make it big." He was not being sentimental and I didn't misunderstand him. I said, "I know you will make it big, but I can't leave now. Later, perhaps I will."

"You know, Margaret, I got a notice to come for permanent work at the Post Office, and I sat in my room and tore it up. Bad as I need money, it was the hardest decision I ever made in my life."

"Well, would you like to be a postman all your life?"

He looked at me and laughed. He didn't need to answer, for he had said more than once, "I want my life to count for something. I don't want to waste it or throw it away. It's got to be worthwhile."

His stop came first and suddenly he grabbed both my hands and said good-bye. That was Friday afternoon, and Tuesday I received his first letter. It was very brief, saying he had arrived Saturday and at first felt strange in the big city, but in a little while he was riding the subways like an old New Yorker. He thought he had a lead on a job—in any case he would try Monday—and meanwhile, I must write him all the news from Chicago and tell him everything that was going on, on the Project; and like every letter that followed, it was signed, "As ever, Dick." I was surprised to get that letter. I never really expected that he would write, but I answered. My letters were generally longer, and I felt sometimes silly and full of gossip, but he continued to write often, if sometimes quite briefly.

In the fall of 1937 he wrote that he was entering the WPA short story contest sponsored by *Story* magazine and Harper's publishing house. I was supposed to enter *Goose Island* myself, but I didn't get it ready in time. Wright had written all four of his novellas before going to New York. When he left he was working on "Bright and Morning Star," which was first published in *New Masses*, but it was not ready when he submitted the manuscript for the contest. "Big Boy Leaves Home" was the only story that had already been published; it appeared first in *American Caravan* while he was still on the Project in Chicago. He had also published "The Ethics of Living Jim Crow" in *American Stuff*. Earlier he had published poetry in *International Literature* and it was in that Russian magazine that both of us first read Mikhail Sholokhov's *And Quiet Flows the Don*.

I don't think Wright ever wanted to write socialist realism, and he chafed under the dictates of the Communist Party to do so. If he had any aspirations beyond that, as he indicated after *Native Son*, it was toward his own unique form of symbolism. I don't think it came as a surprise when Wright won the short story contest, though he had written once that it seemed a long time since he had submitted the manuscript and he hadn't heard anything. His friends in Chicago and New York were pleased and excited, but not surprised. They took it as a matter of course that his work was the best of all those sent in from WPA projects around the country.

In November 1937 I published for the first time in *Poetry* magazine. Wright wrote at once that he had seen the poem, "For My People," written in the summer after he left, and he liked it very much. Meanwhile we were getting things together for *New Challenge* magazine. He wrote that I should send my manuscript of poems somewhere besides Yale. There were lots of other places, he said, and I should give up trying them, for after all they weren't likely to publish me or any other Black person.

In the spring of 1938, *Uncle Tom's Children* was published and Wright won the $500 prize. The book got interesting reviews, but all of them did not make us happy. He had moved to Lefferts Place and was staying with Jane and Herbert Newton. Then, on the wings of success came the news that he was getting married. I hastened to congratulate him, and he denied the whole thing. I learned later that the young, Black, and very bourgeois woman he was dating thought Wright was even more successful in a financial way than he was. He had arranged to rent extra space from the Newtons and move his bride in with them, but her family wanted her to have the best and if he couldn't provide that—no soap. Well, it was no soap. Regardless of financial status, in one year after his arrival in New York, he had achieved national prominence. He remarked in a letter at the end of that year that he had set a goal for five years and one of those years was over. He wanted to write another book right away, a novel, before the first one could be forgotten. Then he wanted to go to Mexico and he wanted to go to Paris.

During the first week in June 1938, I received in rapid succession two airmail special delivery letters. I answered one at once, but before he could receive my answer, he wrote again in great excitement. He said, "I have just learned of a case in Chicago that has broken there and is exactly like the story I am starting to write. See if you can get the newspaper clippings and send them to me." The case was that of a young Black boy named Nixon, who had been accused of rape, and when the police captured him, they forced a confession of five major crimes, of which rape was only one.

I went at once to the offices of the five daily Chicago newspapers to get all the back issues; and I began what lasted a year, sending Wright every clipping published in the newspapers on the Nixon case. Frankly there were times when the clippings were so lurid I recoiled from the headlines, and the details in the stories were worse. They called Nixon a big Black baboon. When I went into news offices or bought papers on the stands, I listened to jeers and ugly insults about all Black people.

Meanwhile, Wright wrote that if I had anything I wanted published to send it to him and he would push my work, as he was now in a better position to help me get published. He had already read many of my assignments on *Goose Island* before leaving Chicago; and he suggested that I might send him more.

Not until Wright visited in November did I learn how he had made use of the newspaper clippings. Actually the case rocked on for about a year. In the fall of 1938, Wright wrote that he would have to make a trip home to Chicago before he could finish the book. One Sunday in November, when I entered the house, my landlady said, "There is a surprise for you in the living room." I said, "A surprise for me? What kind of surprise?" I had come out of a bright day outside and the living room looked dim and shadowy. I squinted my eyes to see and Wright laughed. "Poor little Margaret, she doesn't even know me."

He had only stopped in his mother's house long enough to put down his bag. He washed his hands and ate with us—a quick meal of chicken and biscuits, soup and salad. Then he went out into the streets, visited his friends, the Gourfains, and found a vacant lot to use for the address of the Dalton house in *Native Son*. I thought we were walking aimlessly when we found ourselves at a little tearoom and we went inside. It was late Sunday afternoon—twilight or dusk—and the little bell on the door tinkled to let the keeper know we were entering. There were only two people inside—a man wiping cups and the proprietor; but one knew Wright and we sat down at a table. Soon other men entered; the room began to fill with white men. Gradually I felt acutely that I was the only woman in the room.

Wright explained a little about the new book and told about the clippings. He said he had enough to spread all over his nine-by-twelve bedroom floor, and he was using them in the same way Dreiser had done in *American Tragedy*. He would spread them all out and read them over and over again and then take off from there in his own imagination. The major portion of *Native Son* is built on information and action from those clippings. One of the men asked him where he got the clippings and he looked at me and said, "She sent them to me." A mutual friend, Abe Aaron said, "You ought to dedicate the book to her," and I quickly said, "I'd kill him if he did. He's going to dedicate it to his mother."

Wright said, "How did you know that?" But of course he did. Later he wrote, and I quote:

> I felt guilty as all hell for not writing to you, inasmuch as you had done more than anyone I know to help me with my book. Nearly all the newspaper releases in the book were sent to me by you. Each and every time I sat down to write I wondered what I could say to let you know how deeply grateful I felt.

All in all, Wright was a man of great personal magnetism and charm. Women and men adored him. He could charm the socks off of anyone and everyone he bothered to notice.

He asked me that Sunday if I had a little time to spend helping him find things for the book and I readily assented. On Monday we did several things. First, we went to visit an attorney, Ulysses S. Keyes, who had expressed an interest in meeting Wright and had once asked me to let him know whenever Wright came to town. He was the first Black lawyer hired for Nixon's defense. He had also written a fan letter to Wright, and when we went to his office, he was quite glad to see the author of *Uncle Tom's Children*. I asked him about the Nixon case and if he wasn't the defense lawyer on the case. He said, "I was until this morning. The family has hired an NAACP lawyer, and after I had written the brief and everything." I then asked him if he would give it to Wright. All this time Wright said nothing, and when I asked for the brief, Wright looked at me as if I were crazy and I guess I was, but when we were outside I said, "Well, wasn't that what you needed?" He said, "Yes, but I didn't have the nerve to ask that man for his brief." But of course he found good use for it.

Next, we went visiting Cook County Jail, where Nixon was incarcerated. I nearly fainted when I saw the electric chair for the first time. Outside, we snapped pictures, but I still felt weak. On the elevated train we looked out over South Side rooftops, and Wright explained that he had his character running across those rooftops. I asked why? And Wright said, "He's running from the police." I said, "Oh, that must be dramatic to the point of melodrama." He said, "Yes, I think it will shock people, and I love to shock people!" He grinned gleefully and rubbed his hands together in anticipation, and I couldn't stop laughing.

The next day we went to the library and checked out on my library card two books we found on the Leopold-Loeb case and on Clarence Darrow, their lawyer. The lawyer's defense of Bigger in *Native Son* was modeled after Darrow's defense. Wright was so long sending those books back that I wrote him a hot letter reminding him that I had not borrowed those books permanently! He finished the book early in the spring of 1939, and he wrote that he had never worked so hard before in all his life:

> Listen, from the time I left Chicago and got back to New York, I worked from 7, 8, 9, in the morning until 12, 1, 2 and 3 at night. I did that for day in and day out. Sometimes I worked so hard that my mind ceased to register and I had to take long walks. I never intend to work that long and hard again. If this book is published, then I'll delay getting my next one out, for two reasons: I'm making a new departure and I don't want to kill myself. But I had to get that book out and I wanted it out before the first was forgotten. Rest assured, that if this book is published, you'll hear about it. The liberals, the CP, the NAACP—all of them will have their reservations. Really, I don't believe that they are going to publish it. Really, I don't, even though they've signed the contract. . . .

And again he wrote:

> Yes, I'm beginning another book, but sort of half-heartedly. I'm trying to wait and see what in hell they are going to do with the last one. The title is "Native Son." I don't like the title. They have had it for a week now and I have not heard what they are planning; that is, I don't know if they are going to publish it late Spring or early Fall. The new book will be a sharp departure in my work. I feel that I've gone as far as I care to go with Negro characters of the inarticulate type. Within the next ten or fifteen days I'll hear from Guggenheim. Also I'll know if I can stay at Yaddo, an artist colony, free for a few weeks of rest.

And according to my journal entries I note that he wrote a few days later that he had gotten the Guggenheim! He asked me again about coming to New York and this time, with *Goose Island* finished, I said I was considering it. I have forgotten to say that when he was in Chicago in November, I had discovered the plot of *Native Son* while I was cooking that Sunday afternoon, and I turned to him, stricken, and said, "Oh, we are doing the same thing. The only difference is your character is a man and mine is a woman." He said, "No matter, there's room enough for both," and he buttered another hot biscuit. But I was quite apprehensive and told him so. My fiction was not nearly as well formed and advanced as his, and I felt from that moment that *Goose Island* was doomed. The goose was cooked!

Then, quite without notice, about the middle of May, he turned up in Chicago again for a few days. His younger brother, Alan, was ill with bleeding ulcers and Wright had come to see him. He asked me then about my plans for the trip, and said he would be speaking on Friday evening at the League Convention and hopefully I would be there then. We even discussed riding on the train together, but I said I was not quite ready. I was having real money problems and I did not want to tell him I might not be able to make it. One of the things I promised to do was read the manuscript of *Native Son*, as I had read everything else he had written in manuscript before that, but I never quite got the time. I know I would have violently protested against the end of *Native Son*, although my protests would probably not have helped. I'm sure that was a revised ending. I don't think it was in character for an unconscious character such as Bigger Thomas to analyze his circumstance or situation in such conscious terms. It was obviously a Marxist ending made for socialist realism and not for the naturalistic piece of fiction that *Native Son* is. I can't believe that Wright didn't know that it was wrong, and too contrived an ending.

Wright wrote a piece in *Saturday Review of Literature* called "How Bigger Was Born," and perhaps that character did evolve in his mind for a long time from his childhood and youth in the violent South; but I have told you how *Native Son* evolved from the Nixon case and sociological research done long before Wright began writing his story.

I sometimes ask myself if I had not made the trip to New York that June of 1939, would we have remained friends? I think not. Everything seemed destined toward an end of those three years, for whatever the relationship was worth. At first I was hurt deeply, and pained for many years. The memory of that trip is still too painful to discuss, but as I have grown older and look back in maturity over those three years I know what happened was best for me.

III

Wright's philosophy was that fundamentally all men are potentially evil. Every man is capable of murder or violence and has a natural propensity for evil. Evil in nature and man are the same; nature is ambivalent and man may be naturally perverse and as quixotic as nature. Human nature and human society are determinants, and, being what he is, man is merely a pawn caught between the worlds of necessity and freedom. He has no freedom of choice; he is born to suffering, despair, and death. He is alone against the odds of Nature, Chance, Fate, and the vicissitudes of life. All that he has to use in his defense and direction of his existence are (1) his reason and (2) his will. By strength of reason and will he can operate for the little time he has to live.

His philosophy developed as a result of his experiences: he turned against orthodox religion at an early age because of the religious fanaticism in his family and early home life. He grew up in a South where lynching and Jim Crow and every egregious form of racism were rampant; and the fate of a Black boy was not only tenuous or nebulous, but often one of doom. To be poor and Black in a hostile white world was his first knowledge of the human condition and he found that living in a rural area or in an urban area made no difference. His piece "The Ethics of Living Jim Crow" drives this home long before the autobiography *Black Boy*. The five novellas that eventually form the second edition of *Uncle Tom's Children* were all of one piece: the tragic fate of a Black man in the hostile white world of a violent Southland. The title *Uncle Tom's Children* is a misnomer and misleading. It is an abominable title chosen as usual by the publishers. That book should never have been associated with Uncle Tom. It bears no resemblance to *Uncle Tom's Cabin*, the book or the minstrel play. Any one of the stories would have made a better title for the book. But to get back to the point, *Native Son's* bitterness is even more intense because Bigger is in a bigger bear trap than Bobo and Big Boy. He is in big Chicago, poor, Black, ignorant, and scared! He has no hope of being able to cope with the big white rich man's world in the big city. He blunders into crime. He is driven by such desperate fear he cannot imagine himself as a human being of dignity and worth. He begs the question. He is unconscious, inarticulate, and confused.

Wright developed a cautious and suspicious nature. He said it was part of his protective coloring but that suspicion of everybody grew as he grew older and it was not unlike that of many philosophers who hold secular or materialistic positions. They have no faith in anybody—God, Man, or the devil. He was not nihilistic, but he partook of some of its negativism. He was completely a secularist and secular existentialism was his final belief. It is. best expressed in what I regard as his most autobiographical piece, *The Outsider*. Cross Damon has a lot of Richard Wright in him that Bigger Thomas was not big enough to understand.

All the forces influencing Wright were forces of the white world: He seems to have been shaped very little by Black people. As a matter of fact, Black people were never his ideals. He championed the cause of the Black man, but he never idealized or glorified him. His Black men as characters were always seen as the victims of society, demeaned and destroyed and corrupted to animal status. He was the opposite of what the liberal white man is called: a nigger lover. He probably never reached the point of hating his Black brothers, but he felt himself hated by many of them. Every positive force he recognized in his life stemmed from white forces. Intellectually his teachers and master-models were all white. He was befriended by whites; he was admired and loved more by whites than Blacks. Hatred of the collective white man as a force against the collective Black man was nevertheless coupled with genuine admiration and regard for many personal benefactors who were white. I sometimes wonder if it is malicious to think he would have been happier had he been born white rather than Black. He seemed to feel and believe that all his troubles stemmed from being Black. Unlike Langston Hughes, who loved all mankind and especially his Black brothers, Wright often said that there was no kind of cruelty worse than that which Black people could inflict on their own people. His favorite authors were all white. I cannot think of a single Black author during the thirties whom he considered the equal of any white writer. He had no great respect for the literary achievements of Black people, not even Langston Hughes or W. E. B. Du Bois. Many Black writers admired him, but when he picked his friends among writers, they were all white. He certainly had no high regard for Black nationalism, despite his interests in Africa and Asia. He was not a nationalist but an internationalist.

Wright's greatest influence, however, has been on Black writers. A new school of naturalistic novelists and symbolists, all Black, came out of the thirties and the forties because of Wright. Those most often mentioned are Ann Petry, Willard Motley, Chester Himes, James Baldwin, and Ralph Ellison. I think it is safe to say that, at least in fiction of the twentieth century in Black America, we can mark or date everything before and after Richard Wright. Like the Russians who say they have all come out of Gogol's "The Overcoat," most of our writers have come out of Wright's cloak.

Rereading the early fiction of Wright, one is struck by the passion and the power that always come through. These were also in his early poetry, the remarkable "Between the World and Me" and "I Have Seen Black Hands," two poems he wrote before he turned to Haiku, a form I cannot conceive as being Wright's despite his experimenting in countless poems with it. In his short, factual prose pieces, articles, book reviews, news articles, and potboiling bits of journalism and propaganda, one is always aware of the curious almost mercurial vitality that his writing possessed. Wright really began his imaginative writing career as a poet, although never in his lifetime did he publish a book of poetry. He understood quite well the craft and technique of poetry, particularly free verse. He read and loved poetry purely for enjoyment and relaxation. Once, going on a train trip, he took along Whitman's *Leaves of Grass* to read for pure pleasure. He was quite familiar with the poets of the thirties such as Muriel Rukeyser and Robinson Jeffers. Once he invited me to go with him to hear Kenneth Fearing. He liked T. S. Eliot, W. B. Yeats, Carl Sandburg, Edgar Lee Masters, and even Ezra Pound. He wrote back once from New York how he was reading the "Road to Xanadu," an adventure in the imagination, and also for the first time, *Alice in Wonderland.*

Wright would have been the last person to argue his gift of inner perception, for he also wrote this to me:

> You know, Margaret, writing does not mean that one has a masterful grip on all of life. After all, writing comes primarily from the imagination; it proceeds from that plane where the world and brute fact and feeling meet and blend. In short, a writer may exhibit a greater knowledge of the world than he has actually seen. That may sound like a paradox. . . . This is not irony. Hence, the alertness which should be mine, the sharpness of attention which people say it takes to write, that depth which people find in one's books, well, it simply is not there. . . . I am not subtle, even though there might be imaginative subtleties in my work. Imagination is truer than life; that is the fact which every writer discovers and the fact which people usually concede to the conscious mind of the writer. . . . Frankly, Margaret, what you see and feel in my work is something which everybody has and which, for some reason I don't really understand, gets itself on paper somehow. So don't expect me in my daily relations with folks to have the same strength of vision and awareness you see or think you see in my work. I'm answering this from an odd angle but I feel it is the angle which settles things. I take the world at its face value far more often than you will ever know. Maybe I'll see you again this summer and we'll talk more at length; and I won't be so hurried and worried as I was last time. . . .

The white scholar today who finds Wright a fit subject for study says he cannot understand the apathy of Black scholars toward Richard Wright. What he fails to say is that the Black writer has been profoundly influenced by Wright, impressed with his success, and made confident and bold because of his intellectual honesty. Many Black scholars have in truth written interesting articles, if not books, about Wright, but the Black scholar does not in truth subscribe to the belief that we should bow down before this Black god and worship his Black genius, for some of us have known the man and we know that all men are made of clay.

How I Wrote *Jubilee*

Long before *Jubilee* had a name, I was living with it and imagining its reality. Its genesis coincides with my childhood, its development grows out of a welter of raw experiences and careful research, and its final form emerged exactly one hundred years after its major events took place. Most of my life I have been involved with writing this story about my great-grandmother, and even if *Jubilee* were never considered an artistic or commercial success I would still be happy just to have finished it.

Since its publication, many questions have been raised about my story. How long did it take you to write it? How much research have you done? Where did you find all the material? How much of it is fact and how much fiction? How could a woman like Vyry suffer such outrage and violence and come out of her sufferings without bitterness? Have you put the words of a Nationalist in Randall Ware's mouth? Isn't he ahead of his times? Where did you find proof of free Negroes in Georgia before the Civil War? Were you writing propaganda and deliberately slanting the issues? I hope I can satisfactorily answer these questions for those who are genuinely interested. As for those who insist on their own answers, I cannot hope to change their views.

Minna in my story was my maternal grandmother, Elvira Ware Dozier. When my great-grandmother—Vyry in the story—died, a month before I

This essay was originally published in pamphlet form by Third World Press, Chicago, 1972. Reprinted with permission.

was born, in 1915, grandmother was already in Birmingham waiting with my mother for my birth. Since my grandmother lived with us until I was an adult, it was natural throughout my formative years for me to hear stories of slave life in Georgia. We moved from Birmingham to New Orleans when I was a small child, and my mother recalls how often she and my father came in from night school well past bedtime and found me enthralled in my grandmother's stories. Annoyed, she would ask, "Mama, why won't you let that child go to bed? Why will you keep her up until this time of night?" And grandmother usually answered guiltily, "Go to bed, Margaret. Go to bed right now." My father would add, "Telling her all those harrowing tales, just nothing but tall tales." Grandma grew indignant then, saying, "I'm not telling her tales; I'm telling her the naked truth."

As I grew older and realized the importance of the story my grandmother was telling, I prodded her with more questions: "What happened after the war, Grandma? Where did they go? Where did they live after that place?" I was already conceiving the story of *Jubilee* vaguely, and early in my adolescence, while I was still hearing my grandmother tell old slavery-time stories and incidents from her mother's life, I promised my grandmother that when I grew up I would write her mother's story. I'm sorry she did not live to see the book.

In the fall of 1934, when I was a senior at Northwestern University in Illinois, I thought it was time to put my story on paper. I began writing my version of the Civil War, turning in sections of my manuscript to English C12 (better known as advanced composition or creative writing, under Professor E. B. Hungerford) as my weekly assignments of fifteen hundred words. After three hundred typewritten pages I realized that it did not sound right. At the same time, I was also writing a long poem that was going much better, so I put aside the prose until a more suitable time.

I graduated from college to the WPA (Works Progress Administration), and seven months after graduation I was working on the Writers' Project in Chicago. All kinds of writers, professional and amateur, were working on the *Illinois Guide Book* for WPA subsistence pay. One learned many professional tricks of the trade, if not the actual craft of writing. During those years, I put aside my grandmother's story to write about the near North Side of Chicago, a story about the slums where Negroes were living in increasing numbers in the late thirties.

Sooner than I realized, three years had passed, and in 1939, Congress passed a law saying all boondogglers were wasting the government's money and must get off the WPA if they had been employed for as many as eighteen months. I discovered I was a boondoggler and must get off the government's payroll, and I vowed not to go back to the Project when the necessary interim period of unemployment expired. Instead, I decided I must go back to graduate school and work toward a master's degree in English so that I could go south and teach in a college. I wanted more than anything else to write, but as my father warned me, I would have to eat if I wanted to live, and writing poetry would not feed me. I knew from experience that I would not make a good newspaperwoman, and I could not free-lance and live in the bohemian world. Both worlds produce excellent writers, but by then it was clear that with three generations of forebears who had taught school, I was not going to be able to escape my traditional academic background. (I have now been in the teaching harness for twenty-seven years and as much as I love the profession I have always rationalized that it was only a means to an end, since the chief goal of my life was to be a writer.)

I went to the University of Iowa and studied at the Writers' Workshop there. I wanted my master's thesis to be the Civil War story of my family, but once again my poetry was chosen. Nevertheless, it was at Iowa that I began the long period of research for *Jubilee*. I enrolled in a course in American civilization and was instructed to do three things: (1) Compile and read a long list of books about the South, the Negro during slavery, and the slave codes in Georgia (such books include Ulrich B. Phillips, *American Negro Slavery*; William E. Dodd, *The Cotton Kingdom*; Clement Eaton, *A History of the Old South*; Frederick Law Olmstead, *Journey in the Seaboard Slave States*; and Francis A. Kemble, *Journal of a Residence on a Georgian Plantation in 1838–1839*); (2) Make a thorough study of a Negro woman of the antebellum period; and (3) Learn how to find and use primary sources and documents.

I set myself immediately to the first task, reading Civil War stories and history books. These history books were divided into three classes, according to their viewpoints: (1) history from the southern white point of view, (2) history from the northern white viewpoint, and (3) history from the Negro viewpoint. I was trained as a child in the South to read books at school from the southern viewpoint and books at home from the Negro viewpoint. Once I was out of the South I read more and more from the northern viewpoint. It was amazing to discover how widely these history books differed.

For instance, southern historians claimed slavery was a beneficial system with benign masters; northerners did not oppose slavery as long as it was "contained" in the South and did not spread into the territories; while Negro historians regarded slavery as a cruel, inhuman system. White southerners claimed they fought a war between the states for independence; white northerners claimed it was a rebellion of the southerners against the Union, and Negroes said it was a war of liberation. White southerners claimed Reconstruction was the darkest page in history and a tragic era with Negro rule, while northerners blamed the troubles of that period on the death of Lincoln, on Andrew Johnson, and on ignorant Negroes and Congress. On the other hand, Negroes claimed it was an age of progress, with universal suffrage, land reform, and the first public school system. Then the Ku Klux Klan intimidated and disfranchised Negroes in the counterrevolution to reestablish white home rule. As for Negro rule, my authors reminded me that Negroes were never majority office holders in any state. Faced with these three conflicting viewpoints, a novelist in the role of social historian finds it difficult to maintain an "objective" point of view. Obviously she must choose one or the other—or create her own.

Three years passed before I could get beyond the first historical task assigned to me at Iowa, for I left the university in 1940 with my master's degree and my thesis, the poems, *For My People*. Then in 1942, when *For My People* was published, I visited the New York Public Library's Schomburg Collection of Negro history, on 135th Street in Harlem, for the first time. I found Lawrence Reddick serving as curator of that collection and we renewed a family friendship that dated from his days as professor of history at Dillard University in New Orleans. With his doctorate in history he proved an able teacher of southern history, and gave me excellent leads to Georgia's laws on Negroes. Our friendship and association continue to this day.

In 1944 I received a Rosenwald Fellowship to begin serious research on *Jubilee*. (This came just as I was expecting my first child, so my work was delayed and somewhat handicapped.) At that time I was seeking information about free Negroes in Georgia as well as about my antebellum slave woman. Carter G. Woodson had written a book on *The Heads of Free Negro Families in 1830*, and among those listed was a family named Ware—the name of my maternal great-grandmother. I found that this family might have originated on the Atlantic Coast, in Virginia or the Carolinas. At least they had made early appearances there and may have emigrated to America from the West Indies. Then, as I was reading materials from the congressional investigations of the Ku Klux Klan, I found that one of the victims was an artisan named Ware, who was living in a county adjacent to my story's location. I could not swear that Randall Ware was a member of our family, but one could make a good, educated guess that he was.

Actually I had only recently pinpointed the place for the setting of my novel, for it was not until late in my grandmother's life that I had learned of her birthplace. I said to her one day, rather skeptically, "Oh, Grandma, you don't even know where you were born." And she answered, with the usual indignation that came whenever her story was questioned, "Yes, I do. I was born in Dawson, Terrell County, Georgia."

In 1947, in the course of a speaking engagement in Albany, Georgia, I discovered that I was in the vicinity of Dawson and could make the trip and return to Albany the same day. My grandmother had been dead three years, and I knew no one in Dawson. I went into the colored community and began inquiring about my great-grandparents. I found a man who remembered my great-grandfather, Randall Ware. He said he had lived into his nineties, and had died about 1925. If I wished, the man said, he would show me Ware's smithy, his grist mill, and his homeplace. All this was completely astonishing to me, since I had never known much about Randall Ware except my grandmother's remarks that he was a freeman from birth, that he was a smith who owned his own smithy, that he could read and write, and that he was a rich man. Now I was thrilled to see the smithy with his anvil, his grist mill, and his gingerbread house. I had a camera and tried to take pictures of this anvil on which my great-grandfather had forged a hundred years before, but it was a very gray day and my photography was not expert, so my pictures did not turn out well.

In 1948 I blocked out the story according to its three major periods. (I was living with my husband and two children in High Point, North Carolina, and was idle except for my desultory housekeeping.) For the first time I clearly envisioned the development of a folk novel, and prepared an outline of incidents and general chapter headings. I knew that the center of my story was Vyry and that the book should end with Randall Ware's return. Many of the titles in the book belong to this outline of 1948, such as "Death is a mystery that only the squinch owl knows" and "Freedom is a secret word I dare not say." I anticipated about two hundred fifty such incidents and then reduced them to about one hundred. In essence, I never deviated from that outline. I was beginning to see the story in terms of its own organic growth and wholeness, and I was anxious to put down many of the folk sayings verbatim. Many of these chapter headings are exact repetitions of my grandmother's words.

So, when I say that I have been writing *Jubilee* all my life, that is literally true. It has been a consuming ambition, driving me relentlessly. Whenever I took a job, whether in Chicago in the thirties, in West Virginia and North Carolina between 1942 and 1945, or in Jackson, Mississippi, where I began teaching in 1949, I would hound the librarians to help me find books and materials relating to my story. After I had combed books that I found through card catalogs and reference materials, I sent the librarians on further hunts for obscure items and for bits of information I had picked up here and there. In the course of these searches one of my greatest disappointments came in 1950, when I learned of an excellent collection of books on Georgia and the Negro being offered for sale and was unable to purchase them. There were at least two hundred fifty books and other items, but I lacked the two hundred dollars required. I considered borrowing the money, but it seemed unfeasible in view of family finances, so I had to forget that.

In addition to history books, I was also interested in Civil War novels and any items relating to the period. Although I read most of the prominent Civil War novels of the thirties and a majority of those listed in Robert Lively's *Fiction Fights the Civil War*, these were either from the southern white or northern white point of view. As Lively noted, there was little or no attention paid to the Negro in such works.

Two of my most rewarding experiences came after I received a Ford Fellowship, in 1953, to complete the research on *Jubilee*. In August of that year my husband, our three children, and I were returning from my father's funeral in New Orleans when we decided to make the journey to Greenville, Alabama, and then trace my family's path from there back to Dawson, Georgia. In Greenville, I found my grandmother's youngest, and last-surviving, sister, who gave me a picture of my great-grandmother, corroborated my grandmother's account, and let me see the family Bible and the chest my great-grandmother had carried from the plantation. Later, as we traveled through the Georgia environs of what was my lost plantation, we found an antebellum home near Bainbridge, Georgia, with the square pillars and the separated kitchen-house as described in the story. The lady of the house was kind enough to let me come in and look through her place.

In Dawson, Georgia, I found to my great dismay that a bus depot was now located on the spot where I had seen the smithy and the grist mill just six years before. My husband suggested that I hire an attorney to go into the County Court house and look up my great-grandfather's records. An elderly white attorney whom everybody called "Cap" was most cooperative in this task. When he sent me his findings, they included two legal sheets of paper indicating transfers of real estate from my great-grandfather to wealthy and prominent white citizens of the town. To my amazement all these transactions had occurred during Reconstruction.

Then began another experience in research that paid great dividends. I had first heard of the Southern Historical Collection at the University of North Carolina while I was living in High Point. I was determined to go there. So my family moved to Durham, North Carolina, for six months: husband, children, furniture, books, manuscript, file cards et al. While the children attended school in Durham, my husband drove me to Chapel Hill, and there I delved into the Nelson Tift papers, a collection of account books, diaries, letters, bills of sale, and other personal papers of a wealthy white Georgia planter who had lived in the environs of my story during antebellum days. I spent months with this material, and there are numerous items in *Jubilee* that hark back to the Nelson Tift papers, notably the letter Grimes wrote the master when the slaves had broken into the smokehouse, the conversation among the planters at Marse John's dinner party, and information concerning the two women condemned to hang for the murder of their master and his mother.

When I was not working in the Nelson Tift papers, I was reading slave narratives from the Martin Collection in the library of North Carolina College (later, North Carolina Central University) at Durham. These slave narratives only further corroborated the most valuable slave narrative of all, the living account of my great-grandmother, which had been transmitted to me by her own daughter. I knew then that I had a precious, almost priceless, living document of my own. There are hundreds of these stories, most of them not written, but many of them recorded for posterity. These written accounts tell of the brutalizing and dehumanizing practices of human slavery. They recount such atrocities as branding, whipping, killing, and mutilating slaves. They are sometimes written in the form of letters to former masters, sometimes as autobiographical sketches, and some—like that of Frederick Douglass—have become classics. And all of them contain crucial information on slavery from the mouth of the slave.

What was I trying to prove through this search among the old documents? I was simply determined to substantiate my material, to authenticate the story I had heard from my grandmother's lips. I was using literary documents to undergird the oral tradition.

I visited the Georgia Archives and the National Archives. In both places I was welcomed and assisted by staff members who were not only courteous but interested in what I was going to do with my material. But what *was* I going to do with all this mass of material? How much of the burden of history can fiction bear? I had read piles of material, pored over documents, studied Civil War novels, read history books, and literally memorized books on the technique of the novel while also studying historical novels of English and American literature. In no novel had I read the substance of what I wanted to say.

I went to Yale as a Ford Fellow in January 1954. I spent a semester writing a newly revised version of my antebellum story. By the beginning of May I had two hundred pages of manuscript, but in working with Professor Holmes Pearson, we discovered what I had suspected during my last year at Northwestern: I had a major flaw in my fiction. I knew what it was, but I did not know how to correct it. So I left Yale with Professor Pearson's criticism in my ears: "You are telling the story, but it does not come alive."

In September 1954 I returned to my teaching job at Jackson State College. By then we had a new baby (number four), and my manuscript was stuck in a box in the bedroom closet. For nearly seven years I wrote almost nothing.

Meanwhile, my husband and I concentrated on getting a house for our large family. Then, in the course of those next seven years, we had five bouts with surgery, to say nothing of financial pressures and the steadily mounting demands of a growing family. From 1955 until 1962 I published nothing, and my so-called friends taunted me with the fact that I was not even a has-been, but a might-have-been who no longer produced anything. I did not have time to be irritated by snide comments, but as the Civil War Centennial approached, I grew more and more desperate to finish my story.

The summer of 1960 found my husband and me having surgery ten days apart. But nothing prevented my reading piles of books—nights, Sundays, and holidays. At school I even lectured on the Civil War for our humanities assignments. I was soaked in the period. Meanwhile I had discovered Francis Butter Simkins's *History of the South* and I had purchased W. E. B. Du Bois's *Reconstruction*, because an acquaintance assured me he was the best on the period. I owned Benjamin Quarles's *The Negro in the Civil War*, and had read Charles Wesley's *Collapse of the Confederacy*. When I visited Atlanta University during this period and found Lawrence Reddick as the head librarian, he laughingly chided me and said that I had enough material to write ten books. There was scarcely a tangent I had not explored. As one person asked years later, "Have you done any research on tin cans?" And, funny as that was, by then I had.

In the summer of 1961 I took my two youngest children, ages six and eleven, and journeyed back to Iowa. Once again I knocked on the door of the Writers' Workshop—after twenty years. I talked to Paul Engle, my former advisor, and we began to plan ways and means for me to work toward my doctorate in English, using my novel as a dissertation. Suddenly all the pieces of my life seemed to be falling into place and there was hope for the consolidation of the gains of all the years.

I worked for eight weeks that summer under Verlin Cassill in the Fiction Workshop. He spent painful hours explaining how I was "telling" and not "showing." My first short pieces did not please him at all, but when I showed him the much-revised first chapter of *Jubilee*, to my great surprise he gave it his complete approval. Meanwhile he had taught me how to read the masters of fiction, such as Chekhov, in order to learn how they put their material together. Cassill had not only put his finger on the problem, but he showed me how to dramatize my material and make it come alive. I had never had any trouble with dialogue, but now under his tutelage I was learning how to do close critical reading, and how to make character charts, establish relationships, and control the language more powerfully and effectively.

During that summer I bought a package of specially reprinted Civil War newspapers, northern and southern. Many items in *Jubilee* were lifted from these newspapers with only slight changes of names "to protect the innocent." There were such items as ads for runaway slaves, stories about the munitions workers, Jefferson Davis's speech on the increasing rate of desertions from the Confederate Army, and the failure of Confederate currency. I read S. Wafford Johnson's *Great Battles of the Civil War*, and I listened to recent recordings of Civil War songs. (One of my less attractive tasks was reading the newspaper accounts of boring celebrations in various states commemorating their special historical spots—monuments, places, and battlefields.)

I told myself that I must surely be ready to write the story now. As Reddick had said, I had enough material to fill ten books. My family story could cover five generations of Negroes living in the South. I had a superstructure of facts assembled from word-of-mouth accounts, slave narratives, history books, documents, newspapers; and now I had only to give my material the feel of a fabric of life. At this point I seemed to have a vision of the whole artistic task before me—the creation of fiction from fact, the development of imagined clothing, of muscle and flesh for the real and living bones of history.

In the autumn of 1962 I left my family and teaching position in Jackson, Mississippi, and returned to Iowa to tackle a doctorate in English, and finally finish my book. I went to live in Iowa City, in the home of Alma B. Hovey, a recently retired English professor at the university who had taught composition and the short story for many years. She took me into her home because I really had no place to stay.

At first I was terribly busy, and as usual I had no time to write. I was teaching two classes in freshman English and in rapid succession I was taking the qualifying examination, trying to pass three foreign language requirements, meeting the academic requirements of courses and seminars for the degree, plus reading a long list of books for the comprehensives. This went on for two years, including one semester in which I had to write 135 pages of seminar papers. I was so happy to have the opportunity that I worked furiously, but I was also tense and fearful that I would become ill or run out of time and money before I could even get to my manuscript.

Gradually I began to relax. I had found myself in the house of a Alma Hovey, who was perpetually serene, busy, optimistic, and encouraging. Something of her spirit seemed contagious. "One thing at a time" was her first admonition, and finally I took it so seriously that we reached the point where she actually had to prod me through those awful Latin translations. Regularly she insisted on my drinking a cup of coffee in the morning before facing the Iowa weather and stopping in the afternoon to relax over a cup of hot tea. I found myself in the house of a friend.

It was not until the fall of 1964, however, that I completed my written and oral comprehensives and once again could turn to the novel. I needed leisure, and money to provide that leisure, for a year. Twice before, I had received fellowships for *Jubilee*. Now I borrowed my salary from Jackson State College and the state of Mississippi in order to buy what I needed most, time to write without worry. I mortgaged my soul "to the Company Store." When the comprehensives were over and I had secured a dissertation committee, I returned home to my husband in Jackson and voted in the 1964 presidential elections. Then I went to New Orleans to spend five weeks with my two younger children in my mother's house. They had been there throughout my sojourn in Iowa. During those five weeks, I rewrote and revised again the two hundred pages of the manuscript that covered the antebellum section.

Thus far most of my writing had dealt only with the antebellum period. Aside from the last chapter, which was part of the first version, I seemed to dread tackling that most important of all periods, the middle section and the Civil War. My job was threefold: (1) to hew to the line of my simple folk story during the war, (2) to maintain historical accuracy, and to relate the importance of the war to my characters, plus (3) to point up the significance of the Negro people and their role during the war.

In January 1965 I wrote for the first time the Civil War section of the book. In the library at Jackson State College my friend the reference librarian found copies of the old *Century Magazine* with "Battles and Leaders of the Civil War," the famous references that Stephen Crane used in *Red Badge of Courage*. I kept a hot line open to her for two or three weeks until I returned to Iowa City at the end of the month.

Miss Hovey and two of her friends were standing on the icy platform when I disembarked there from the frozen train. For the next two and a half months I was to find everything I needed in her house to finish *Jubilee*. Miss Hovey had in her possession a book of songs published by Oliver Ditson nearly a hundred years ago. This collection contained Civil War songs, Stephen Foster songs, Negro folk songs—including spirituals, work songs, popular tunes, and even minstrel songs and favorites I had heard my grandmother say that my great-grandmother had sung. I had long since appropriated the haunting, "Flee as a bird to your mountain," but the hair rose on my head one Sunday afternoon when I saw at last a song I had hunted for, for years, "I'll be there, I'll be there, when the muster roll am calling I'll be there." In addition this book contained the famous "Kingdom Coming" and "Babylon Is Falling," as well as "Marching through Georgia." With Horace Greeley in the attic and my brand new paperback copy of Harry Hansen's *The Civil War*, a new one-volume history, in my hands (along with the picture books I had borrowed from the library), everything was finally perfect and every piece of the giant jigsaw puzzle was falling into place.

I had always had the fear that before I could finish the book, Verlin Cassill would be out of the Writers' Workshop, and that winter he suddenly began to threaten to leave. Some six weeks passed before a dispute in the Workshop had cooled down enough for Cassill to look at my manuscript. Meanwhile I was sick with apprehension and fear over the possible departure of my key faculty reader. But just as I thought it would drive me to physical illness, Miss Hovey decided that she would read each page I wrote. Then we discussed it in terms of the whole story and she commented and made suggestions, either approving or disagreeing. That saved the day. By February 22, 1965, I had completed the second section, that terrible Civil War— which my husband declared he had been fighting all the twenty-odd years of our marriage. I celebrated by going to the movies and going out with friends to dinner.

In March came the word of approval from Cassill and Vance Bourjaily, and I began to race toward graduate-college deadlines. I gave the first section out to be professionally typed while I undertook to revise the second section and begin work on the third. With all the stops out I began to drive toward the finish, and at last, what I had always hoped would happen began taking place in that third section. All the story I had known and lived with for all my life began to pour out on paper as fast as my fingers could type. I worked from seven in the morning until eleven and stopped for lunch, or whenever Miss Hovey stopped me; then I went back to the typewriter and worked in the afternoon until supper or tea at four and then after supper until eleven o'clock. I pushed myself beyond all physical endurance, and in two months, I was happy to lose twenty pounds. On the morning of April 9, 1965, at ten o'clock, I was typing the last words, "Come biddy, biddy, biddy, Come chick, chick, chick." And I was grateful to God and everybody who had seen me through to that moment.

But the end of the first draft is not by any means the end of the writing. I believe that writing is nine-tenths rewriting. Since I write almost nil in longhand, and since my fingers on the typewriter never go as fast as my thoughts, I always write too much and too easily and therefore I must always cut, cut, cut and revise many times. A first draft is only the beginning.

A writer is fortunate if he has an editor to do the first big scissors-and-paste job for him. I do not know how many times through the years the first part of the novel had been revised. The final version bears very little resemblance to my first draft, except that it began as always with Hetta dying when Vyry was two years old, and the manuscript always repeated the same incidents of the flogging through Randall Ware's return to take Jim away. One major revision entailed reorganization for me, cutting out all the heavy expository and purely historical passages. This freed the story of unnecessary burdens. Another revision tackled only language and dialect, in which every word of dialect had to be changed for spelling and modernization. In these two respects the thesis copy in the University of Iowa Library bears no resemblance to the printed copy. The final polishing of *Jubilee* was for me the least satisfactory of all jobs, since it was done in a hurry. Such a revision usually involves tying in all the transitions, straightening sentences, cutting out clichés, and "'taking out the whiches'." I hope I'll write other books, and next time I'll try to do better. I really think I can.

People ask me how I find time to write, with a family and a teaching job. I don't. That is one reason I was so long with *Jubilee*. A writer needs time to write a certain number of hours every day. This is particularly true with prose fiction and absolutely necessary with the novel. Writing poetry may be different, but the novel demands long hours every day at a steady pace until the thing is done. It is humanly impossible for a woman who is a wife and mother to work on a regular teaching job and write. Weekends and nights and vacations are all right for reading, but not enough for writing. This is a fulltime job, but for me, such full attention has only been possible during the three Depression years I was on the Writers' Project and during that one school year in which I finished *Jubilee*. I enjoyed the luxury.

How much of *Jubilee* is fiction and how much fact? When you have lived with a story as long as I have with this one, it is difficult sometimes to separate the two, but let us say that the basic skeleton of the story is factually true and authentic. Imagination has worked with this factual material, however, for a very long time. The entire story follows a plot line of historical incidents from the first chapter until the last: the journeys, the Big Road, the violence, the battles, the places Vyry and Innis lived and the reasons they moved.

I had very little to go on, however, with my white characters, and many of them are composites. The middle section of the story is my most highly imagined section, since I had only fragments that had to be pieced together. The entire white family is obviously symbolic of the Confederate South, from the death of the master, who was sure the Union didn't have a leg to stand on, until the death of the mistress in the face of the complete collapse of the Confederacy. The young master and Lillian are both part of this larger symbol.

I always intended *Jubilee* to be a folk novel based on folk material: folk sayings, folk belief, folkways. As early as 1948 I was conceiving the story in terms of this folklore. I also wanted the book to be realistic and humanistic. I intended this twin standard to prevail, and I wanted as well to press the leitmotiv of the biblical analogy of Hebrews in Egypt with folk in America. I had always known that Negro slaves prayed for a Moses to deliver them from Pharoah. For instance, Brother Ezekiel is in the tradition of the slave preacher who was conductor on the Underground Railroad, who preached of our deliverance through a God-sent Moses, and who also served as a spy in the Union Army, doing all he could toward gaining our freedom. In the section of the book called "Reconstruction and Reaction," Vyry echoes this theme when she says she knows people must wander a while in the wilderness. Like all freed slaves they believed they were on their way to the Promised Land.

Insofar as Vyry's lack of bitterness is concerned, maybe I have not been as honest as I should be, taking the license of the imaginative worker, but I have tried to be honest. My great-grandmother was a definite product of plantation life and culture. She was shaped by the forces that dominated her life. In the Big House and in the Quarters, she was raised according to Christian ethics, morality, and faith, and she could not react any other way. Her philosophy of life was a practical one, and she succeeded in getting the things she wanted and prayed for. She realized that hatred wasn't necessary and would have corroded her own spiritual well-being.

But Randall Ware was not of the plantation life and culture, and he could not be shaped by such forces. He belonged to an artisan class of free laborers and had neither the slave mentality of Innis nor the caste notions of Vyry. He was bitter because he was frustrated. He did not get what he wanted, and he was conscious of how he had been cheated. He was forced to sell his land; he failed to get his political rights as a free citizen; he was shamed into a kind of cowardice at the cost of his life and manhood, and he was even denied the pleasure of seeing his children grow. He could not be expected to think or act in any way like Vyry or Innis. My mother says she knows—according to my grandmother and great-uncle—that Randall Ware was a militant man in his lifetime. I have not used him to place the words and ideas of the 1960s and a Nationalist in his head. So I am equally proud of my heritage from both my great-grandparents. For if Vyry was quite a woman, Randall Ware was also quite a man.

Obviously my philosophy of history is radically different from either the southern white or northern white point of view. It is exactly what one would expect it to be, a point of view. I believe that the Civil War was inevitable, that, in the words of William Seward, it was an irrepressible conflict brought on by great economic, political, and social forces of change. I believe that slavery was a real and central issue causing the war, that Negroes played a vital role in the war, that the emancipation of the slaves worked concretely toward the winning of the war by the Union. The war was in every sense a bloody revolution, since nothing before the Civil War was ever the same afterward. Every aspect of American life was changed. The democratic promise of liberty and freedom was destroyed during Reconstruction by the counterrevolution of the white South, through the use of the Ku Klux Klan and with the tacit consent and agreement of the Bourbon South and the industrial North. Throughout the whole chain of events the Negro was a pawn, and he remains such today. We are a minority group with a subculture and we are unrecognized by the dominant culture. I try to be realistic. Which authors have influenced me the most? Cassill recommended Chekhov, but I was even more concerned with Tolstoy's *War and Peace*. There were passages in that novel that I read over and over, not only because I think it is the greatest book on the subject and of its kind, but because there were so many parallels made by a great master to the situation I was using— the serfs on the land, the aristocracy, nineteenth-century warfare, the intense religiosity, and the great panoramic scenes as well as the wonderful close-ups. Cassill also recommended Sir Walter Scott, and I found him most useful because of the popular character of his novels and their strong folk flavor. Always the great novels of peasant people such as Knut Hamsun's *Growth of the Soil* and Pearl S. Buck's *Good Earth* seemed to be close to the kind of story I envisioned in Negro folk literature. Some of Steinbeck's stories are like that, such as *Tortilla Flat*. Balzac I had read long ago, but not while writing the novel. Faulkner I reviewed in his entirety because of his total concern with the southern experience.

For the technique of the novel, I found studies made by James Warren Beach in his *Twentieth Century Novel* quite relevant, and I was also forced to read Henry James. I bought, of course, Cassill's book *Writing Fiction* and read it from cover to cover, but then who is the greater teacher, the book or the man? For the particular category of Civil War novels, Robert Lively's *Fiction Fights the Civil War*, and *The Historical Novel* by George Lukacs I found indispensable for philosophy and point of view. I have Lukacs to thank for an understanding of the popular character of the historical novel; for the recognition that I was among the first dealing with characters looking up from the bottom rather than down from the top; and for an understanding of Abraham Lincoln as a world historical figure who was always a minor character seen through the mind of the major characters.

I was also very much intent on showing the interrelationships of class as well as race and on keeping in mind how these interrelationships shape the political, economic, and social structure in the entire panorama of the novel, just as they do in real life. Color, caste, and class were equally as important as race. I had long been aware of how this worked in fiction.

On the problem of verisimilitude in the novel, I recognize the fact that I was constantly faced with the difficulty of taking real and consciously chosen Negro characters like Randall Ware and Henry McNeil Turner and making each of them point up his historical significance, while at the same time shaping them into fictitious characters of my imagination. I am sure I follow a long line of predecessors in this. In terms of these realistic demands on the story, I think of my work as a mixture of what the twentieth century realists, naturalists, and symbolists all do.

Life itself is the standard, but not a dull copy of life, rather a bold and completely new creation of simulated life, a world I make, people I devise, situations I imagine, and motives I develop. This is my world of make-believe, of "let's pretend," with material from chaotic and disorganized life and experience. My characters look like and talk like and act and think and react like human beings, but in reality they are only the fictive creatures of my imagination. Their language and their actions are familiar, their world is familiar, and they move toward a definite point in reality, but they are people in a world of imagination. They are so real, so intensified, that I become involved with them, so exaggerated that they seem of exact human proportions, and I struggle and suffer with them. But their ultimate reality is one of verisimilitude, for my novel is a canvas on which I paint my vision of my world.

Margaret Walker, c. 1985; photo: Robert Townsend Jones, Jr.

Part Two:
Literary and
Other Legacies

A Literary Legacy from
Dunbar to Baraka

Paul Laurence Dunbar

I cannot remember when I first heard the poetry of Paul Laurence Dunbar (1872–1906). It seems I have known it all my life. My mother read the dialect poems to me when I was a small child, although she must have been still a little girl herself when Dunbar died. I must have discovered his nondialect poems later at school, but they, too, were familiar throughout my adolescence. I memorized at least a half dozen of the dialect poems as part of my own speaking repertoire for church socials and school programs.

When I bought my second copy of Dunbar's complete poems, I was deep in civil war research and I realized that the plantation dialect of Dunbar's poetry was authentic antebellum southern speech. His dialect poetry also contains a great deal of homespun philosophy typical of the slave and the slave mentality. It is not only for their humor, but also for their insight into folkways, folk speech, and folk beliefs that Dunbar's poetry is a treasure house for that period in Black American history now more than a century old.

This essay has been compiled from a variety of speeches or essays prepared to celebrate the writers discussed on different occasions, including the centennial celebration of Paul Laurence Dunbar's birth, held in Dayton, Ohio, in 1972; a special tribute to Langston Hughes at the Dusable Museum of Afro-American History in Chicago, in 1968; a chapter in an unpublished book on James Baldwin; and a conference on Amiri Baraka in Jackson, Mississippi, in 1987.

Looking back today on Dunbar's life and times, there is much we can learn of his tragic dilemma as a poet and as a Black man. For a very long time white America considered him the only Negro poet and treated him condescendingly. He realized that the white world in the United States tolerated his literary genius only because of his "jingles in a broken tongue," and they found the old "darky" tales and speech amusing and within the vein of folklore into which they wished to classify all Negro life. This troubled Dunbar, because he realized that white America was denigrating him as a writer and as a man. The dialect poems are, however, not a reflection on the dignity and the self respect of the Black people they represent. The attitude of whites toward Dunbar's poems reflects, instead, another vein of racism. It is a racism that rejects the genius of Dunbar as a poet, and as a man preeminently. Today Dunbar's poems are beginning to appear in new anthologies of American literature. [1]

The Black scholar has repeatedly criticized Dunbar for his sentimentality and his too-easy facility for versifying. There was a period in the life of Black America when Dunbar was just as unfashionable as the spirituals, and some Black people still reject the dialect poems as the mark of an Uncle Tom or a toadying both to the white man and to the infamous slave period. One objection Black scholars make to Dunbar is that he was an accomodationist and not a writer of social protest. Saunders Redding and Arthur P. Davis said he avoided anything that might antagonize white America. [2]. This may be true, but it is also a fact that Dunbar lived in a time when the minstrel show and the plantation tradition were all America was willing to accept of Negro artistry. Dunbar knew this and he is, therefore, a creature of his times.

I think, for my generation, Dunbar was also seen as not only representative, but exemplary. Born into a family of freed Blacks who had a vivid and immediate sense of their slave heritage, Dunbar was able to take full advantage of the opportunities available to Blacks in the years following the war. Viewed by today's standards, he might have been a child prodigy. He began reading early, using the Bible as his text, and he earned the reputation for skillful oratory in elementary school. His literary and verbal skills were honed during high school when Dunbar, the only Black person in his elementary school to gain admission into Dayton's single high school, became an active participant in debating societies and served as editor of his school paper. His public writing career was already off to a glowing start and his name, a household word in his hometown by the time of his high school graduation.

It was then that Dunbar's troubles started. He was destined to become a writer, but he was Black and the best he could do was to find a job as an elevator boy at a local hotel. Through a stroke of luck, he was given an opportunity to welcome a group of professional writers at a local conference. This resulted in broad national exposure and the publication of his first volume of poetry, *Oak and Ivy* (1893).

Soon Dunbar was traveling among a community of actors, Black intellectuals, and writers like himself, having launched his writing career full time with another volume of his poetry *Majors and Minors* (1895) and regular appearances in the major literary magazines of the day. When William Dean Howells read and reviewed *Majors and Minors*, Dunbar's reputation was set and his two volumes *Oak and Ivy* and *Majors and Minors* were reissued together as *Lyrics of Lowly Life* (1896), with an introduction by Howells. Howells did nuch to establish Dunbar as the "dialect poet of Black America," and Dunbar found, to his dismay, that though he was in great demand in the Black community, he was not free to realize the full range of his talent.

Dunbar was our first truly successful professional Black writer. His travels, speaking engagements, and productivity made him an international figure. He rose to fame quickly, and just as quickly, he was in decline, for before he reached his thirty-fourth birthday, he was dead of consumption.

It is perhaps too much to make a general and absolute statement that Dunbar is at his best in the dialect poems when we remember such pieces as the remarkable "Ere Sleep Comes Down to Soothe the Weary Eyes" or any of his pungent and bitter stanzas such as "We Wear the Mask," "Life," "Sympathy," and so forth. But I think it fair to say Dunbar has made a unique contribution to American culture and literature with his dialect poems. They not only represent an age never to be recalled, but they are still fresh, vivid, and entertaining.

What William Dean Howells said in his introduction to Dunbar's *Lyrics of Lowly Life* is essentially true: Dunbar expressed a side of Black life aesthetically and with great skill for the first time in Black American literature and history.

Langston Hughes

For thirty-five years Langston Hughes (1902–1967) was my friend and mentor. I saw him first in my teens in New Orleans, Louisiana. He was reading his poetry one February night in 1932 at New Orleans University, now Dillard, where both my parents were teaching. My mother was the music teacher and both my mother and father were on the Lyceum Committee.³ The white president had told my father that Langston Hughes was seeking an engagement in New Orleans and his fee was only one hundred dollars, but the president did not believe as many as one hundred people would come to hear a Negro read his poetry, even if he had published six books. I overheard my parents discussing this and I said, "You've just got to have him because I have never seen a real live poet." Then my mother said to my father, "See if he will come on a sixty–forty basis. We might not be able to raise a hundred dollars." But we did. We wrote eight hundred letters to people all over the city, and as the result of this and all kinds of other publicity, a thousand people packed the school auditorium to hear the famous poet. That night was one of the most memorable in my life because he also read some of the poetry I had written. It must have been awful stuff, but he said it was good. And then he told my parents they must get me out of the South so that I could become the writer my talent promised. I was sixteen and was halfway through college, although Langston thought I was still in high school.

The next school year (1932) my parents enrolled my sister and me in Northwestern University, outside of Chicago. At Northwestern, I heard Dr. W. E. B. Du Bois speak, and after his lecture I went up to him, introduced myself, and told him I wrote poetry. He invited me to send him something for *The Crisis* magazine, published by the National Association for the Advancement of Colored People. In May 1934, my first poem in a national magazine appeared in *Crisis*.

After my graduation from Northwestern, Langston Hughes introduced me to Richard Wright. Wright was presiding over the Writers' Group of the National Negro Congress in Chicago, when I first met him. At that meeting also was Arna Bontemps, to whom Wright subsequently introduced me. Later, when the League of American Writers met in New York in 1939, I saw Langston and Wright at the New School for Social Research. It was there I also first met Sterling Brown and his wife, Daisy, and there Langston introduced me to Waring Cuney.

In 1942, when *For My People* was announced by Yale as the winner of that year's Younger Poets Competition, Langston wrote a letter of congratulations, which I still have. He did the same thing in 1966, when *Jubilee* was announced. I don't think any other Black poet or writer did, but it was like Langston to encourage writers, and it is the first legacy we have from him. Langston gave me many autographed copies of his books, perhaps sixteen. He was always encouraging me to grow in the wonder of poetry. He also gave me other poets' works such as a copy of Gwendolyn Brooks's A *Street in Bronzeville.*

I remember that first night in New Orleans when my sister, Mercedes, and I were talking in bed about our wonderful evening, and she said, "Do you think you'll ever see him again?" "Oh sure," I said airily, "he'll probably ask me out to lunch, and we'll have him in for dinner." True enough, Langston came to dinner many times in various places: New Orleans, the Grand Hotel in Chicago, and New York. He visited me in Boston; High Point, North Carolina; and Beaumont, Texas. And I was his guest both at 83 St. Nicholas Place and 220 East 127th Street in New York. He and I ate with Arna Bontemps in chop houses, and in 1943 we spent six weeks at Yaddo.

I received letters and cards from Langston mailed from all around the world from Spain, and Africa, and Carmel-by-the-Sea, in California. He came to Jackson for a week in 1952 during our Literary Festival.[4] When Wright died in Paris (1963), it was Langston who wrote me from London, telling of his last visit in Wright's home. I saw Langston for the last time in October 1966, at a party for the poet Leopold Senghor, in New York. Langston looked pudgy, but his smile and bear hug were the same. I could not believe my ears in May 1967, when I heard over the radio that he was dead. For weeks it was impossible either to face or discuss his death, but I think each time I return to New York I miss him most. I never imagined what it would be like not seeing Langston in New York.

Although he was born in Joplin, Missouri, and grew up in Lawrence, Kansas, and Cleveland, Ohio, Harlem was his home. New York was especially *his* city. His poetry, plays, and fiction, as well as his autobiographies, are flavored with the language, the body tang, and the street culture of New York City. The Harlem Renaissance, of which he was so indubitably a part, as a leader and catalyst, was only the beginning of Langston's love affair with Harlem. As a superb folklorist, writer extraordinaire of the Black American experience, Langston captures the character, mood, and appearance of Harlem. More than that he was part of this place he called *home*, this place he loved and celebrated in poetry and prose. Typical of this celebratory style is "Harlem Night Song":

Come,
Let us roam the night together
Singing.
I love you.

Across

The Harlem roof-tops
Moon is shining.
Night sky is blue.
Stars are great drops
Of golden dew.

Down the street
A band is playing.

I love you.

Come,
Let us roam the night together
Singing. [5]

Shakespeare in Harlem: This was Langston Hughes. His love for Harlem and its people was genuine, and he fully understood the paradox of race and class that led to his ironic poem "Minstrel Man":

Because my mouth
Is wide with laughter
And my throat
Is deep with song,
You do not think
I suffer after
I have held my pain
So long?

Because my mouth
Is wide with laughter
You do not hear
My inner cry?
Because my feet
Are gay with dancing
You do not know
I die? [6]

Our literary legacy from Langston Hughes is tremendous. Arna Bontemps told me two weeks before he died that Langston left eighty-six literary works including an unpublished third volume of his autobiography. Only W. E. B. Du Bois has left a larger body of work, and he lived thirty years longer than Langston's sixty-five years.

As a poet, Langston gave poetic and folk expression to a new Black idiom, which was quite different from Paul Laurence Dunbar, Sterling Brown, or James Weldon Johnson. Dunbar expressed the language and life of the plantation Negro, whereas Sterling Brown expressed the roustabout, the

Black worker, and the strong Black hero in legend and fact. James Weldon Johnson gave us the Black folk preacher, or the sermon tradition, in *God's Trombones*. Langston has immortalized the modern culture of the city streets, the menials, the domestic servant, the Jesse B. Simples with their homely philosophy, even the so-called bum on the corner, the displaced homeless, demoralized, dispossessed, and denigrated human beings who huddle on the streets of northern cities. I think one of the best monuments to Langston is a line from his poetry that is written in stone on the City Hall of Lawrence, Kansas, where he was a young boy: "We have tomorrow before us, bright like a flame."

Langston Hughes's emergence in the 1920s, which I consider the true decade of the Harlem Renaissance, was more than accidental. He wrote instinctively in the poetry and prose typical of that decade and shared the belief that Black people were exotic, primitive hedonists who, despite suffering and persecution, were simple people "Not without Laughter." "The Negro Speaks of Rivers" (1921), *The Weary Blues* (1926), *Fine Clothes to the Jew* (1927), *Not without Laughter* and *The Dream Keeper* (1932) grew out of that decade, as did *The Ways of White Folks* (1934).

During the 1930s Langston's writing was very different from that in the Harlem Renaissance. It was the decade of the Great Depression, and writers were guided by the stream of social protest. Langston wrote plays, poetry, and fiction that mirrored the underlying bitterness of racial suffering, deprivation, and dehumanization. Hughes's versatility and the importance he placed on fusing social and artistic concerns can be seen in the play *Don't You Want to Be Free* (1939), from the Suitcase Theatre, and an early play, like *Mulatto* (1935), which had the longest run of any Black play on Broadway up to that time, and in his poetry such as "Good Morning Revolution."

The forties and the war years were, for Langston, the beginning of the long lists of newspaper columns, as well as the "Madame" poems and his autobiography, *The Big Sea* (1940). His poetry was abundant during this period, and he collected them mostly for his volume, *Shakespeare in Harlem* (1942). Through Jesse B. Simple, Hughes had access to an entire nation of Blacks above and below the Mason-Dixon Line. Simple's first appearance in the *Chicago Defender* newspaper sought to elevate ordinary Black folk.

Despite being called by the McCarthy UnAmerican Activities Committee, Langston was going strong in the fifties, during the Cold War years. He was writing more poetry, more plays, and more fiction, and publishing more books of different kinds. He collected his "Simple" columns and brought them out as a series of books, including *Simple Takes a Wife* (1953) and *Simple Stakes a Claim* (1957). He wrote his stories during this period on the culture and literature of Black America and the West Indies.[7]

Although a number of his musical productions went to Broadway in the 1950s,[8] perhaps his most financially successful theatrical work was *Street Scene*. The script was based on Elmer Rice's 1947 play of the same name. Langston's lyrics were set to music by Kurt Weill.

In the sixties Langston joined the Black Arts Movement and was, like Marcus Garvey in the 1920s, one of the first to say and celebrate "Black is Beautiful."

Perhaps no other writer has been more famous, and yet, more misunderstood in terms of his legacy and literary contributions than Langston Hughes. Literary critics downgraded his poetry as too simplistic and *not revised ever*, but they could not say that about his fiction, surely the result of very careful craftsmanship. His friend, Richard Wright, believed Theodore Ward was a better playwright than Langston, but it is clear that Langston was more prolific, had longer runs, and won more prizes. Now, years after his death, we are gradually realizing the genius and literary stature of Langston Hughes.

It is impossible to contain in a capsule the personality of Langston. The rich, warm, racy, charming, ebullient Langston can only be understood by those who knew him personally. He had a wonderful even-tempered disposition, a rare sense of humor, a contagious love of humanity, and at the same time a keen intellect. Practical and disciplined, he worked steadily at the craft and art of writing. Rising at noon, having breakfast at 3:00 P.M. and then going downtown to Broadway or the Village at 6:00, returning after midnight and writing till daylight, this was his day. His apartment and study had complete organization of manuscripts, books, papers. He was a thoroughly organized man—inside and out.

He has bequeathed to us—the Black People of the world and all humanity caring, listening, and reading his works—he has bequeathed to us a rich and powerfully significant body of literature: trenchant, folksy, moving, and meaningful. Our Brother Langston, you sleep now with the immortals. How glad I am that you walked and lived among us and that you were for little me—My Precious Friend!

James Arthur Baldwin

James Arthur Baldwin (1924–1987) was born in Harlem, New York City, the oldest of nine children. His father was a lay-preacher in the Holiness-

Pentecostal sect. His grandfather had been a slave. At age fourteen, Baldwin was ordained a preacher in this church. At eighteen he graduated from Dewitt Clinton High School, and at twenty-four he left for Europe on a Rosenwald Fellowship. Meanwhile, he had met Richard Wright, who encouraged the young Baldwin to become a serious writer. With the aid of a Eugene Saxon Memorial Trust Award, he wrote his first novel, *Go Tell It on the Mountain* (1953). In Europe, he completed two books: *Notes of a Native Son* (1955) and *Giovanni's Room* (1956). Returning to America after nine years abroad, he became known as the most articulate literary spokesman for the civil rights of the Negro people. In one famous quotation Baldwin remarked that all the emerging African nations would be free before a Black man in America could buy a cup of coffee.

Although it is true that Baldwin is known best as a master of the essay form, with six novels to his credit he must also be considered a major novelist. Three definite influences dominate the fiction of James Baldwin: (1) his father as a stern religious fanatic (alternating with a father image of Richard Wright); (2) the spiritual and sexual conflict between his religious background and (3) the human condition of homosexuality. These conflicts provide the tensions of his major prose work. Always displaying a painful sensitivity to the phenomenon of race in America, compounded by his experience of homosexuality and religion, Baldwin's prose is characterized by a style of unusual beauty and telling power. The novel *Go Tell It on the Mountain* reveals an exceptional understanding of the feeling and tone in the religious and folk expression of Black people. The threshing floor scene is memorable for this, and despite the lack of organic unity, this first novel is a masterpiece. An obvious conflict, or cleavage, in Baldwin's own personality is revealed in much of the autobiographical prose. Baldwin communicates and allows us to witness his inner agony in a singular fashion. There is constant conflict between Black and white, between God and the devil, between the flesh and the spirit, and there is also an appealing repetition of the overlapping of sexual and religious emotion in the curious blending that seems most authentic when it is also most subtly conveyed.

His language seems deliberately chosen in order to shock and disturb, to arouse, to repel, and to shake the reader out of complacency into a concerted state of action. There is ghetto language, yes, but his verbalization of Black life at all levels is not limited to the guttersnipe.

Baldwin's themes are repeated over and over: the terrible pull of love and hate between Black and white Americans; the constant battle of one possessed by homosexuality between his sense of guilt and ecstatic abandon; the moral, spiritual, aesthetic, and ethical values such as purity of motive and inner wholeness; the gift of sharing and extending love, inner grace, beauty in the eye of the beholder; the charms of goodness versus evil, an inner ear to hear the disturbing social upheaval; and the rewarding ecstasy of artistic achievement. Such values are in constant warfare with racism, industrialism, mechanistic and dialectical materialism (including sensuality and mammon); there is, in fact, a global power struggle. Everything demeaning to the human spirit is attacked with vigor and righteous indignation.

Characters in Baldwin's novels and short stories almost always include himself. He is the young boy preacher Elisha in *Go Tell It on the Mountain*. He is the first person singular in *Giovanni's Room*. He is both Caleb and Leo Proudhammer in *Tell Me How Long the Train's Been Gone* (1968) and he is Rufus in *Another Country* (1962). In the poignant love story *If Beale Street Could Talk* (1974) and in *Little Man, Little Man* (1976), he is again a protagonist and in *Just Above My Head* (1979) he is alternately Hall Montana and his brother Arthur. Puppet and king, he is lord of all he surveys; omniscient as God and wrathful as the Old Testament Yahweh. Baldwin's point of view is always dramatically centered in himself with the exception of *Go Tell It on the Mountain*. *A Dialogue* (with Nikki Giovanni) (1973) and *Rap on Race* (with Margaret Meade) (1971) have the same format. They are what they say: conversation pieces dealing with a variety of subjects—writing, women, race, the social scene, but chiefly race.

As a playwright, Baldwin's first two published plays reveal an uneven talent. *The Amen Corner* (1968) is artistically successful. Similar in tone to *Go Tell It on the Mountain*, it communicates the religious emotion of the Holiness-Pentecostal Sect. The second play, *Blues for Mr. Charlie* (1964), has a definite social message but is not as successful artistically as a play. But the minor flaws here, as in all of Baldwin's works, are outweighed by his major achievements. Baldwin proves the growing contention that twentieth-century American literature has been most feelingly or effectively expressed by Afro-Americans.

If Beale Street Could Talk and *Little Man, Little Man* seem both an interlude between the earlier and later novels and a prelude to the monumental work *Just Above My Head* (I hear music in the air). Among his books this last is the most powerful, the most profound. The themes are the same: gospel music as it expresses religious emotion and fervor of Black people; homosexual love; explicit in its every detail; and racial cleavage, symbolized by terror, death, incest, and tragedy. But there are some differences. His women characters are more believable than in previous novels. Julia is not a shadow but a well-conceived, realized, and rounded character. So are the two mothers. Baldwin is no longer the young virtuoso. He is the mature master, at peace with himself, coming to terms with life. He no longer rails against the problem of evil in the world. His symphony of life deals both with polyphony and cacophony. He knows that innocence and corruption may exist together. Here in this latest novel there is no obvious cleavage. He has gotten everything together and the elements in the book coalesce with no loss of lyricism, poignancy, or power.

Baldwin is also a preacher. He is a defender of the faith. He comes straight out of the Old Testament prophets, a Jeremiah writing for white America. His book on the child murders in Atlanta, *The Evidence of Things Not Seen* (1985), is really a sermon. He takes his text from Hebrews, chapter 11, verse 1: "Now Faith is the Substance of things Hoped for, The Evidence of Things Not Seen." And he proceeds to develop the homiletic plot as a narrative art form found in a religious sermon. He begins in the midst of disturbing social conditions, then analyzes the causes or reasons for the lack of equilibrium in the racial climate, at the same time showing how and why a discrepancy exists between the actual and the ideal. He moves quickly to a denouement, or resolution, of the conflict and then applies the consolations of religion as a panacea, and finally, predicts dire consequences if humans do not heed the warnings and the solace of the Divine. Baldwin is a preacher!

His collected essays are sermons. Baldwin chose to bring the earlier volumes together—*Notes of a Native Son* (1955), *Nobody Knows My Name* (1961), and *The Fire Next Time* (1963) in *The Price of a Ticket*. Perhaps he knew that this would be his last opportunity to use his hell fire and damnation themes to exhort an American nation to its knees. By permitting us to witness his oracular prose sermons just one more time, Baldwin forces us to confront the radical honesty that few can claim. Ruthless, he spoke the terrible truth to us all. He wrote passionately, beautifully—about things that did exist for him as a Black man, an expatriate, a homosexual, a creative artist, and a rebel. Through the expressions of this one man, Black folk and white folk can perhaps look more truthfully at themselves and one another. There is no question that James Baldwin is a very significant American writer whose immortal place among the literary giants of all time is definitely assured.

Amiri Baraka

Somewhere else I have written of the genius of Amiri Baraka, born Leroi Jones (b. 1934). I have likened him to the picaro and his work to the picaresque. But in the broad spectrum of his accomplishments, this is not enough. Fifteen years ago in New York at the Black Academy of Arts and Letters, I presented Baraka with the Literary Award for that evening and I said then that when our people look backward from the twenty-first century, they will see and remember the genius of this man, who by the time he was thirty had made monumental strides and significant artistic achievements. He is poet, philosopher, political theoretician, and tactician. He is also novelist, dramatist, and essayist, anthologist, teacher; and perhaps his proudest claim to fame is being the father of seven.

But what I believe is most important is to understand his world-view, or the synthesizing vision that he has provided for the twentieth century. No matter how you consider Baraka, you must confront his creative genius. Whether you begin with the grade school boy writing comic strips or the high school boy interested in drama and taking roles in school plays, or see the college student—first at Rutgers, then at Howard, studying philosophy—you are dealing with the uncommon stuff of genius. Most of all, he is the picaro, the rascal, the devil, the Uriel of Black Literature. I say he may be like a chameleon changing colors as he changes roles from one period to another. I say primarily these periods and colors are white, Black, and red. In his autobiography, he says he has also been brown with a streak of yellow. I prefer to deal with the three periods, white, Black, and red.

Leroi Jones went from college to the armed services and the Second World War. He returned home in the early fifties and became a part of the Beatnik crowd in Greenwich Village. There he and his first wife published a magazine, *Yugen,* in which many of his beatnik poems first appeared. This was his white period: white job, white wife, white publishers, white success. He belongs to the same group of poets writing beatnik poetry on the East and on the West Coast. These writers include Allen Ginsberg, Bob Kaufman, Jack Kerouac, and Laurence Ferlinghetti. Tinged with a political radicalism and sophistry, the poems of this period reflect a nihilistic philosophy and the canon of dadaism in post-World War II artists. Racism is not the chief ingredient, but disillusionment with the absurd realities of the times, and a rebellion against the status quo in favor of the way out. The philosophy was expressed in an early song, "Hallelujah, I'm a Bum." Baraka's title poem, "Preface to a Twenty Volume Suicide Note," reflects this sensibility in no uncertain terms.

> Lately, I've become accustomed to the way
> The ground opens up and envelopes me
> Each time I go out to walk the dog.

Or the broad edged silly music the wind
Makes when I run for a bus . . .

Things have come to that.

And now, each night I count the stars,
And each night I get the same number.
And when they will not come to be counted,
I count the holes they leave.[9]

But when the era of the sixties began, Leroi Jones changed colors and did a left about-face. He became Black. He left Greenwich Village and the white wife, white success, white life, and his beatnik self, and went uptown to Harlem. There he was involved with the Harlem Youth Center, funded by the government. Here he was accused of using government funds to develop racially separate Black Nationalist groups. In 1964, he was awarded the Obie (an Off-Broadway award) for his revolutionary Black drama, *Dutchman*.

Then he went home to Newark, New Jersey. During one of the Black urban rebellions of the period, the "Newark Riot" of 1967, Jones was arrested and charged with carrying a concealed weapon. He was beaten and kicked and brought before a judge who sentenced him to three years in jail (no bail) and a $25,000 fine. The judge cited one of Jones's poems, "Black People," declaring it obscene and therefore he was justified, he said, in imposing a stiff fine and penalty. But the poster picture of Leroi Jones, with a white bandage on his beaten Black head, appeared all over the country, and the $25,000 was quickly raised. Paying the fine, he was given a suspended sentence of three years.

In Newark, Leroi Jones became Imamu Amiri Baraka, the leader of a Kawaida sect of the Muslim faith and the founder of Spirit House, where revolutionary Black drama flourished. Throughout, he was a prolific writer, the author of more than a half-dozen books of poetry, including *Preface to a Twenty Volume Suicide Note* (1961) and *The Dead Lecturer* (1964), *Black Music* (1967), *Blues People* (1963), as well as *Home: Essays* (1966), *The System of Dante's Hell* (1965), a novel, and at the end of this period, an anthology called *Black Fire* (1968), produced in collaboration with the brilliant Larry Neal, who had also co-edited the Black drama issue of *The Drama Revue*[10] in which several Black playwrights and their plays first appeared. Among them were Ed Bullins, Ron Milner, Sonia Sanchez, Jimmie Garrett, Ben Caldwell, Marvin X, John O'Neal, and Baraka himself.

In Newark, Baraka also became interested in the political process. He worked for voter registration and was largely responsible for the election of his old friend, Kenneth Gibson as the first Black mayor of Newark. Later they fell out over money problems for a housing project and became bitter enemies. This was chiefly due to their political differences, since Baraka became more revolutionary and Gibson more bourgeois.

In 1976 Baraka changed colors and periods again. He went to Tanzania and the sixth Pan-African Conference, where he became interested in the Pan-African theories of the socialist leader, Julius Nyerere. He came home a Red, converted to scientific socialism and chiefly the Marxist-Leninism of Mao Tse-tung. In the Sunday, October 17, edition of the *New York Times*, Baraka detailed this new phase of his development. Immediately branded a Communist, he encountered new political difficulties in his writing and teaching profession. His books went out of print and he could not get published. He was indicted on a charge of beating his Black wife, and jailed on Riker's Island.

What is significant in all these changes is the continuing vision of Baraka in poetry, politics, and philosophy. He is concerned with a people's world, a democracy in reality, a world of social justice, freedom, peace, and human dignity. Beauty and truth are synonymous with these. Racism, fascism, and sexism are triple evils in such a scheme. And jail seems to ripen the writings and vision of many. In 1983 Baraka and his wife, Amina Baraka, collaborated on a volume of poetry by Black American women called *An Anthology of African American Women: Confirmation*. He wrote the introduction, which is a historical overview of Black women writing in America since the days of Phillis Wheatley.

In 1984 Baraka's *The Autobiography of Leroi Jones* appeared. One of the important features of this book is his language, the Black dialect of his own youth and times. He makes an addition here to the long list of Black writers who have experimented with the Black idiom in English, including Dunbar's plantation dialect, Langston Hughes's street-culture speech of Harlem, Sterling Brown's roustabout, and Zora Neale Hurston's southern patois. Baraka's vision is a Black vision in poetry and in drama, in politics, or philosophy, where he combines Humanism, Pan-Africanism and Marxism.

A volume of essays, *Daggers and Javelins* (1984), sums up this threefold vision of Baraka in philosophy, poetry, and politics. Here he traces the revolutionary line of militant Black writers from the slave narratives of Frederick Douglass through the nineteenth-century Black nationalists and the Harlem Renaissance to the Black Arts Movement of the sixties and the seventies (which he led), and including the great Black figures and leaders— W. E. B. Du Bois, Langston Hughes, and Richard Wright. Baraka's vision places him in the company of these men. This is a great humanistic tradition from the oral folk roots of Black culture to a Black radical, or Pan-African nationalism and revolutionary internationalism. Baraka's threefold vision is an all-encompassing vision for the twentieth century and the Black world.

Notes

1. e.g., Richard A. Long, and Eugenia W. Collins, eds. *Afro-American Writing* (University Park, Pa.: Pennsylvania State Press, 1985); and others.

2. See introductory note on Dunbar in *Cavalcade: Negro American Writing from 1760 to the Present*, ed. Arthur P. Davis and Saunders Redding (Boston: Houghton Mifflin, 1971), pp. 205–06.

3. Lyceum Committees, common in Black colleges, planned cultural programs and events for the campus and surrounding community in which the college was based. This was one of the major avenues for Black artists or other distinguished individuals to gain access to Black communities, especially in the segregated South.

4. Held at Jackson State University, this was the first of many such festivals organized by Margaret Walker. Typically, it brought national and international artists together, served as a forum for new poets (like Alice Walker in 1973) and other artists, and eventually led to a number of writers' workshops in the Jackson area and throughout Mississippi, perhaps the most famous of which was the Free Southern Theatre.

5. Langston Hughes, *Selected Poems* (New York: Knopf, 1971), p. 61.

6. Sterling Brown, Arthur P. Davis, Ulysses Lee, eds., *The Negro Caravan* (1941; New York: Arno Press, 1969), p. 370.

7. *The First Book of Negroes* (1952); *Famous American Negroes* (1954); *First Book of Rhythms* (1954); *The First Book of Jazz* (1955); *Famous Negro Music Makers* (1955); *The Sweet Flypaper of Life* (1955); *A Pictorial History of the Negro in America* (1956); *The First Book of the West Indies* (1956); *Famous Negro Heroes of America* (1958); *The Book of Negro Folklore* (1958).

8. According to James Emmanuel, the *Barrier*, based on "Father and Son," and *Mulatto* began their run on Broadway in 1950. *Simply Heavenly* appeared on Broadway in 1957. Hughes pioneered what became the "gospel play." He generally wrote the script and lyrics collaborating with another musician.

9. Leroi Jones, *Preface to a Twenty Volume Suicide Note* (New York: Totem/Corinth, 1961), p. 5.

10. This issue of *The Drama Review*, 12:4 (Summer 1968), signaled the rise of the Black Arts Movement in many ways, as it was the first appearance of Larry Neal's seminal essay on the subject.

The Education of a
Seminal Mind,
W. E. B. Du Bois

Any man who lives ninety-five years gives cause for celebration. When such a man has influenced his century, this is double cause. William Edward Burghardt Du Bois (1868–1963) was a seminal mind who influenced the twentieth century. He is one of five great thinkers of our age. These five men are Albert Einstein, Sigmund Freud, Karl Marx, Soren Kierkegaard, and William Edward Burghardt Du Bois.

In the third world, and the Black world, Pan-Africanism is the idea fostering unity, peace, and human dignity. W. E. B. Du Bois is the father of Pan-Africanism. How did such a mind develop and what is the lesson we learn, the legacy we inherit from this great seminal mind of our age?

As Du Bois has written himself, "I was born by a golden river and in the shadow of two great hills."[1] Great Barrington, Massachusetts, in the valley of the Housatonic and the Berkshires, was his birthplace on February 23, 1868. He went to school in the little town where he lived, and when he went to high school he followed a college preparatory course that included algebra, geometry, Latin, and Greek. He graduated at the top of his class in 1884, but it was fall of the next year before he went to college, and then it was to Fisk University in Tennessee, where he had a scholarship rather than to Harvard, which he had had early dreams of attending first. In Nashville, at Fisk, he

This essay is adapted from a speech delivered to the National Association of Black Behavioral Scientists in Jackson, Mississippi, in 1968.

discovered for the first time a world of beautiful Black people, another culture, and a different racial atmosphere. He fell in love with this Black world and ever thereafter the romance endured.

For the next nine years—from 1885, when Du Bois was seventeen, until 1894, when he was twenty-six—he studied at Fisk, Harvard, and in Berlin. At Fisk, his grades qualified him for Phi Beta Kappa, but he did not receive his key until nearly fifty years later, since Black colleges were not members of the Phi Beta Kappa organization. After graduation he became a teacher and worked for a brief time in the rural schools of Tennessee. At Fisk, he had heard the spirituals sung for the first time by his fellow students; in rural Tennessee, he saw something of the Black church and a community that he had heretofore witnessed only in a limited fashion.

He eventually took three degrees from Harvard, receiving the bachelor's in philosophy (cum laude) in June 1890, and returning to work on his master's in the fall. In 1892 he went to Berlin for two years before retuning to Harvard again, where he received his doctorate in 1896. Looking back on his Harvard years for a moment, we recognize many of the great names among his teachers. He studied psychology under William James and philosophy under Josiah Royce and George Santayana; with the latter he read Kant's *Critique of Pure Reason*. He became one of James Bushnell Hart's favorite students in history, and he studied composition under Barrett Wendell, and perhaps Milton, Chaucer, and Shakespeare under George Kittredge. Other noted scholars there at the time were Francis Child, Charles Eliot Norton, Justin Winsor, John Trowbridge, William Goodwin, and Frank Taussig. Professor Nathaniel Shaler asked a white southerner to leave his class in geology because he objected to sitting next to Du Bois. Albert Bushnell Hart guided Du Bois through his graduate courses and started him on his work in Germany.

During all this time, Du Bois had concentrated on history, English, and philosophy, but more and more he was inclined toward the social sciences and particularly sociology. But no such discipline existed either at Fisk or Harvard, nor in Berlin.

Thus far his papers and oral examinations had been concentrated in history. On taking his bachelor's degree, he had given an address on the president of the Confederacy, Jefferson Davis. His graduate work was the basis for his *Suppression of the African Slave Trade* (1896), the scholarly work that became volume one in the Harvard Studies series, edited by Harvard's President Charles Eliot Norton.

Teaching seemed his only possible career, and his first opportunity came from Wilberforce College in Ohio. Here, he was not allowed to teach that strange new social science, the discipline sociology. Hence, after a year in Ohio, where he married, he accepted a position as assistant instructor at the University of Pennsylvania, for the handsome sum of $900 for the academic year. He ignored the "pitiful stipend," as he called it, because for the first time he could make a scientific study of Negro life. *The Philadelphia Negro* (1899) is the product of research based on interviews with 5,000 people, covering the two-hundred-year history of the Negro in Philadelphia.

Perhaps you may imagine his education had ended. He had spent more than eighteen years in classrooms as a student and had two baccalaureate degrees, a master's, and the equivalent of two doctorates, but in a seminal mind like Du Bois's, education begins at birth and lasts till the grave. His teaching career was marked by constant research and experimentations.

During his two stays in Atlanta—covering the years between 1897 and 1910, and 1934 and 1944—Du Bois began to indicate his intellectual depth and his creative and scholarly achievement. Under his direction, the humanities and social sciences flourished. He left Atlanta the first time to become editor of *The Crisis* magazine, which he founded (1910). When he returned to Atlanta, he founded *Phylon: The Atlanta University Review of Race and Culture* (1940). Many young Black writers appeared in the pages of *Crisis* and *Phylon* and the list of Afro-American writers and authors who published work there reads like a Who's Who in Afro-American Literature. Du Bois was certainly one of those elder statesmen who with Charles S. Johnson, James Weldon Johnson, and Alain Locke presided as godparents to the great Harlem Renaissance of the 1920s.

Three major contributions of W. E. B. Du Bois to scholarly learning and the intellectual milieu of the twentieth century are not only part of our legacy from him, they are part of his own continuing education. They reveal his inquiring mind and his great creative and scholarly genius but they also reveal most his dedication to his people, the Negro race, or those dark-skinned descendants of Africa and citizens of the African Diaspora and their struggle for freedom, justice, peace, and human dignity.

Du Bois was a founding member of the Niagara Movement, out of which came the National Association for the Advancement of Colored People. He was also the Father of Pan-Africanism, a global institution and philosophy for the unity, freedom, and dignity of all Black people. He helped organize the World Conference for Peace and attended a half-dozen conferences for peace. He attended five Pan-African congresses. At the end of his life he was directing and editing an encyclopedia of the Negro, on a global scale.

In addition to all these activities, he wrote and published twenty-one books; edited fifteen volumes in the Atlanta University series; and wrote another hundred pamphlets, essays, and articles. These books and papers represent the product and the education of a seminal mind. And what of his relevance to the issues of today?

Sociology in the twentieth century really began with W. E. B. Du Bois. The great protest movement in the struggle for civil and human rights, for peace and racial justice—this too, was led by W. E. B. Du Bois. Revolutionary Black nationalism began in the nineteenth century, and Pan-Africanism is the philosophy that best expresses the unity, humanity, and search for freedom incipient in that Black nationalism. Du Bois is the key to every modern concern, idea, and movement dealing with race.

As to his poetry and fiction, most of us present are familiar with *The Souls of Black Folk* (1903), in which he extols the three great gifts of Black folk: brawn and brain and creativity or soul and spirit. Few are as familiar with his poetry and prayers and his novels for and about his people. They have inspired all who have read them: *Dark Water: Voices from within the Veil* (1920); *The Dark Princess: A Romance* (1928); *Black Reconstruction in America* (1935); *Dusk of Dawn: An Essay toward an Autobiography of a Race Concept* (1945); *The World and Africa: An Inquiry into the Part Which Africa Has Played in World History* (1947); and the Black Flame Trilogy, including *The Ordeal of Mansart* (1957), *Mansart Builds a School* (1959), and *Worlds of Color* (1961).

Two poems are my tribute to the great seminal mind and education of Dr. W. E. B. Du Bois. The first is "Giants of My Century":

Du Bois, I know you well
Brother of my flesh, my kith and kin;
Race of my Race, man of Humanity.
They could not hope to know
how seminal your mind was for us all;
the seeds of truth, of destiny, and love
were sown by you; your broken dreams
evolving ever higher into realms
beyond the earth and sea into a land
where we are gods and touch divinity.
Make me a monument for five men:
Marx and Freud
Einstein, Du Bois, Kierkegaard
and build no more.

They have their feet upon the floor
of ocean sand
and their heads are above clouds.
They are the giants of my century.
Their words are prophecies
lighting our decades.
Their smiles are rainbows
arching the planet's globe.
When they sing
cadences of love songs and music of machines
lullabies in the night
break our dread existence into luminous day.

These are the men who marshalled aeons of satellites;
planetary stars and galaxies yet unborn.
These are the doctors, nurses, midwives ushering our birth.
Our umbilical cord is wasted in the vapid dawn
of prehistoric time
hidden in caves of gargantuan mists.
And they were there.[2]

The second poem is "Five Black Men":

Douglass, Du Bois, Garvey, King, and Malcolm X
Five Black men whose leadership we cherish
in the history books
from Slavery to Segregation and the Age of Integration
down the primrose path to face oblivion

Five Black Men . . .
And ten will save the city

Douglass was the first
brooding face upon our dark waters rising out of twilight
clutching stars
daring the sun
casting light from all ages
on our miserable circumstances.
Yes, we know our Black brothers in Africa
sold their mothers and sisters into slavery.
Yes, we know our white brothers in Europe
packed us like sardines in cans on their stinking ships

and we died like flies.
"I have known the curse of slavery
and the masters' cruel will
the overseer's lash and the reveille at dawn;
when the freedom talkers came
they called my name
but I was not on the roll of the chained
nor the dead
lying before the merciless pity of the yankees.
I was long since gone.
Lincoln and Garrison
John Brown and the Alcotts
they were all the same—
aflame with one true mockery
of freedom, truth, and faith
but not for brotherhood.
I tell you my fellow shackled human race
we must strike the first blow.
We must be free
by the blood of our own humanity."

Five Black Men . . .
and ten will save the city.

Du Bois was Renaissance . . .
Ancient Egypt, Thebes, and Memphis
Cush and Temples of Karnak, Luxor, and Parthenon
They were his temples too.
He stood astride the chasm of yawning worlds
bridging the centuries
holding bolts of lightning
electric in his fists.
First social doctor of our century
analyzing our lives, our cities, our towns and schools;
loving our people
and understanding
how western man built his system
on the labor of our lives
cheap labor, slave labor, from dusk till dawn;
how they made a myth out of race
joined it to their christianity
and annihilated our lives.

Du Bois reminded us and prophesied:
"The problem of the twentieth century will be the color line."

Five Black Men . . .
and ten will save the city.[3]

Notes

1. W. E. B. Du Bois. *Darkwater* (New York: Harcourt, Brace, 1920), p. 5.

2. Reprinted from *This Is My Century: New and Collected Poems by Margaret Walker* (Athens: University of Georgia, 1989).

3. Reprinted from *This Is My Century.*

Rediscovering Black Women Writers in the Mecca of the New Negro

Various scholars are responsible for perpetuating two or three serious misconceptions about the Harlem Renaissance: one that it was centered on Harlem and a coterie of writers living there; two, that it was an exclusively male movement; and, three, that it began before the twenties and lasted well into the forties. The Harlem Renaissance was neither entirely about Harlem nor entirely about the lives of that emerging Black community; it was not exclusively male; and third, it was completely limited in philosophy and ethos to the decade of the twenties, the Jazz Age, the golden twenties. Perhaps the most serious misconception is the notion that women were absent from or inconspicuous in the movement. More than a dozen women were an integral part of that decade. They were poets, playwrights, novelists, singers, and dancers, and their successful enterprises were noteworthy. These women included Jessie Redmon Fauset (1882–1961), Georgia Douglas Johnson (1886–1966), Anne Spencer (1882–1976), Zora Neale Hurston (1903–1960), Nella Larsen (1893–1963), Alice Dunbar Nelson (1875–1935), Angelina Weld Grimké (1880–1958), and Gwendolyn Bennett

This previously unpublished essay was conceived and partly written in the early 1970s, before the current surge in interest in Black women writers, past and present. Parts of this essay were presented by Maryemma Graham on behalf of Margaret Walker at a 1985 conference on the Harlem Renaissance, at Hofstra University, Hempstead, New York. The editor wishes to thank Mae Henderson for her suggestions on preparing this essay.

91

(1902–1981), who all died before their importance to the movement could be reevaluated. Helene [Hubbel] Johnson (1907–), Dorothy West (1908–), May Miller (1899–), [Mary] Effie [Lee] Newsome (1885–), are fortunately still alive, and can witness a new era of interest in their life and work.

Why do we have such a low profile and image of these women? The subordinate status of women is one answer, the racial identity of these women is the second, and the repression of women by the dominating males in the movement is a third one. But neither Langston Hughes nor Arna Bontemps could totally overshadow the irrepressible and talented Zora Neale Hurston, and she is now always remembered as part of the Renaissance.

Although largely unheard during the twenties, with that decade's emphasis on what she called being "tragically colored," Zora Neale Hurston, born in "a Negro town," gloried in her Blackness, and set out to follow her mother's advice to "Jump at de sun." Whatever the theme or the content, the contribution of this most productive of the Renaissance women cannot be obscured. Hurston brings to the period a spirit of creativity and insight that has often been underrated and sometimes overlooked. Although she wrote short fiction throughout the twenties, her major works did not appear until the 1930s. In this respect, Hurston signals the end of the Renaissance period, but in spirit and content, she is very much of it. She heralds a new era of development in Afro-American literature, especially in her use of folklore and her treatment of the Black community. She used language to generate and emphasize a sense of community among Afro-Americans. Author of collections of folklore, poems, plays, articles, and novels, Hurston was quite prolific in the early part of her career, but her works seemed to have gone out of print as quickly as they appeared. They include: *Jonah's Gourd Vine* (1934); *Mules and Men* (1935); *Their Eyes Were Watching God* (1937): *Tell My Horse* (1938); *Moses, Man of the Mountain* (1939); *Dust Tracks on a Road* (1942); and *Seraph on the Suwanee* (1948). Her biographer, Robert Hemenway, lists some eighty published works, and thirty-four unpublished materials in his "Checklist of Writings."[1]

Throughout her novels, the element of folklore is a constant companion of the soulful, real, "feeling" characters that Hurston magically creates. In the 1970s a new and burgeoning interest in Hurston began to surface in literary circles, and in the authenticity of certain aspects of her writing. *Their Eyes Were Watching God*, in particular, has become the focus of much of this praise, not withstanding the negative treatment the novel received after its publication in 1937. Condemned by Richard Wright as a socially unaware display of "ministrel technique," *Their Eyes Were Watching God* stood, and continues to stand, for so much more than the work was originally given credit. The novel deals with womanhood in a fresh, realistic, and even revolutionary way by acknowledging the desire for female independence and individuality.

Nella Larsen, author of *Quicksand* (1928) and *Passing* (1929), runs a close second to Hurston both in skill and success, but many forget that Jessie Fauset precedes the Renaissance and is at once a forerunner and a part of the Harlem Renaissance. Fauset worked in *The Crisis* magazine office with W. E. B. Du Bois and was author of four major novels: *There Is Confusion* (1924), *Plum Bun* (1928), *The Chinaberry Tree* (1931), and *Comedy American Style* (1933).

Georgia Douglas Johnson was the author of three books of poetry: *The Heart of a Woman* (1918), *Bronze: A Book of Verse* (1922), and *An Autumn Love Cycle* (1928), and a prize-winning play on Broadway, *Plumes*.[2] The highly imagistic title poem of *The Heart of a Woman* expresses intense longing and suppressed creativity:

The heart of a woman goes forth with the dawn,
As a lone bird, soft winging, so restlessly on,
Afar o'er life's turrets and vales does it roam
In the wake of those echoes the heart calls home.
The heart of a woman falls back with the night,
And enters some alien cage in its plight,
And tries to forget it has dreamed of the stars
While it breaks, breaks, breaks on the sheltering bars.[3]

The Heart of a Woman has also been described as a "book of tidy lyrics that express the love-longing of a feminine sensibility,"[4] suggesting that while Johnson was in tune with popular conceptions of womanhood, she also expressed what might be called a pre-feminist consciousness.

In her next work, *Bronze: A Book of Verse*, Johnson becomes a spokesperson of Black race, speaking of its woes and concerns. Consequently the dominant image throughout this work is the "mantle" symbolizing the "cloak of darkness" borne by the members of her race.[5] This volume, however, is considered less important than her first volume, probably because *Bronze* came to life because Du Bois criticized her slight attention to race in *The Heart of a Woman*. *Bronze*, then, was to become her "race" volume. In 1928 Johnson's *An Autumn Love Cycle* was successfully published. It continues in the vein of her previous poetry, discussing a woman's feelings from the beginning to the end of a love affair. Many feel that this volume parallels one of Johnson's own romantic affairs. *An Autumn Love Cycle* has endured as Johnson's best volume of poetry.

Johnson's poetry was probably not so well known as her plays, probably because her 1927 play, *Plumes*, won first prize in the *Opportunity* magazine competition that same year. *Plumes* tells the story of a Black family stuck between the proverbial rock and a hard place. The mother of a fourteen-year-old daughter, deathly ill, has to decide whether to spend the fifty dollars she has saved on an operation for the ailing child or, in the face of her seemingly imminent death, on the best funeral in town, complete with "plumed horses." A folk element is revealed in the mother's distrust of medical doctors.

Two earlier plays by Johnson, *Blue Blood* and *Popoplikahu*, both appearing in 1926, show evidence of her preoccupation with the theme of miscegenation, due perhaps to her own mixed ancestry. I tend to agree with Gloria Hull that Johnson's drama must be far more seriously considered if we are to have a true critical assessment of her work.[6]

The current revival of interest in Alice Dunbar-Nelson adds greatly to our understanding of this woman, a shadowy figure despite her preeminence in the period. She was mostly known as the wife and widow of Paul Laurence Dunbar, whom she married in 1898.[7] A poet and writer in her own right, her writing career had begun early in life, with a book of short stories, *Violets and Other Tales* (1895) published when she was only twenty years old. In 1899, through the aid of her husband's agent and publisher, *The Goodness of St. Rocque*, a second volume of short stories was published to accompany Dunbar-Nelson's *Poems of Cabin and Field*. Instances such as this served to establish Alice Dunbar-Nelson as an author in relationship to her husband, rather than autonomously.After her estrangement from Dunbar, another phase of her life began. During this time, for example, Dunbar-Nelson, who was an English teacher for much of her life, founded a local chapter of the Circle for Negro War Relief, while serving as an active member of the Republican Party, and head of the Anti-Lynching Crusaders. All the while she maintained her writing career, although not often for adequate compensation. Thus, much of her writing manifested itself in journalism relating to the causes in which she was involved. Her column entitled, "Une Femme Dit," which treated such areas as Black theatre, the progressiveness of the Black church and its clergyman, and American politics, appeared regularly in Black newspapers. Not a foreigner to poetry, her contributions in this area gained her a seat in the halls of the Harlem Renaissance writers. "Summit and Vale," "A Common Plaint," and "Sorrow's Crown," are a few examples of her poetic verse.[8]

With the exception of novelist Dorothy West, most of the remaining women published poetry, mainly in magazines. Seven anthologies, as well as *The Crisis* and *Opportunity*, should be consulted for their work.[9] Other journals that published Black women writers include the special issue of *Survey Graphic*,[10] edited by Alain Locke, and the short-lived *Fire!!* and *Ebony and Topaz*.[11]

Among these women Anne Spencer should be considered a major poet of the period.[12] James Weldon Johnson claimed the honor of discovering her. He says in his brief introduction to Spencer that "she was the first woman to show so high a degree of maturity in her work. She is less obvious and less subjective than any of her predecessors than of any other Negro poet."[13] Surely no other woman writer of the Renaissance won such praise from her male contemporaries. She was vitally connected to four well-known men: W. E. B. Du Bois, James Weldon Johnson, Sterling Brown, and Langston Hughes, all of whom visited and stayed overnight with the Spencers. Sterling Brown and Langston Hughes both wrote poems to Spencer. And yet, Spencer, who wrote prolifically, is little remembered today. In her poem, "Dunbar," she not only echoes the famous poet, but seems to have known, if not sealed, her own fate.

> Ah, how poets sing and die!
> Make one song and Heaven takes it;
> Have one heart and Beauty breaks it;
> Chatterton, Shelley, Keats and I—
> Ah, how poets sing and die![14]

Gwendolyn Bennett was a well-trained artist and poet with Marxist political leanings. She was a native southerner, although she spent much of her early life in New York. She had extensive training, which can be attributed to both American and Parisian art schools. Bennett, like many other artists, was introduced to the Harlem Renaissance by James Weldon Johnson, and maintained an active association throught her monthly literary and fine arts column that ran in *Opportunity* for almost two years. Bennett's literary career was very brief, and we have an assortment of poetry, one short story, a few essays, and her delightful columns in *Opportunity*.[15]

Effie Lee Newsome was also a participant in the Renaissance, although she did not live in Harlem. She published poetry in *The Crisis* and *Opportunity* from 1917 through the 1930s. She bacame editor of "The Little Page," the children's section of *The Crisis*, while her husband fulfilled his responsibilities as an African Methodist Episcopal minister. Her career as a children's author/librarian and teacher followed her moves from Wilberforce University, in Ohio, to Birmingham, Alabama.[16] Newsome has left her mark mainly as a children's writer; her volume of poetry for children, *Gladiola Garden*, was published in 1940.[17]

Angelina Weld Grimké, Helene Johnson, and Dorothy West were all from the Boston area. Born into a famous family, Grimké was the daughter of an interracial marriage, which was as much a family tradition as was the concern for racial justice. Grimké was educated in the tradition of the New England elite and prepared herself for a career as a teacher, which began in Washington, D.C. According to Gloria Hull, Grimké began writing very early, and what we know of her life is mostly extracted from her poetry and her diaries.[18] Her early play *Rachel*, which was produced in 1916, indicates that there was not only an active literary community in Washington, where the play was first performed, but suggests that Grimké was herself a harbinger of the Renaissance, which was only later identified with Harlem. *Rachel* was a truly Black play in that it addressed racial issues and depicted the situation of Blacks in America.

Much younger than Grimké, Helene Johnson and Dorothy West came to young adulthood in a Boston that had a thriving Black literary community. They were both educated in the schools of Boston and became active members of Boston's Black literary club, the Saturday Evening Quill, which published an annual anthology by the same name. Johnson and West moved to New York around 1926—during the heart of the Renaissance—to begin their journalism studies at Columbia University. Once in New York, Johnson sold what was probably her first published poem "Bottled: New York," which appeared in *Vanity Fair* magazine in the May 1927 issue. I was impressed with the sharp pictures she drew of Black urban life in the poem:

Upstairs on the third floor
Of the 135th Street library
In Harlem, I saw a little
Bottle of sand, brown sand
Just like the kids make pies
Out of down at the beach.
But the label said: "This Sand was taken from the Sahara Desert."
Imagine that! The Sahara desert!
Some bozo's been all the way to Africa to get some sand.

And yesterday on Seventh Avenue
I saw a darky dressed fit to kill
In yellow gloves and swallow tail coat
And swirling a cane. And everyone
Was laughing at him. Me too,
At first, till I saw his face
When he stopped to hear a
Organ grinder grind out some jazz.

Boy! You should a seen that darky's face!
It just shone. Gee, he was happy!
And he began to dance. No
Charleston or Black Bottom for him.
No sir. He danced just as dignified
And slow. No, not slow either.
Dignified and proud! You couldn't
Call it slow, not with all the
Cuttin' up he did. You would a died to see him. [19]

I imagine that this poem was Johnson's official initiation into the Harlem Renaissance. She had much success with her writing after this: she placed third in an *Opportunity* literary contest, her poetry was well represented in the major Black anthologies of the period, and in her hometown publication, *The Saturday Evening Quill*, Johnson was represented by five poems in one of its annual issues.[20] She eventually returned to Boston, probably after the official end of the Renaissance in 1929, and was heard from infrequently after that.

Dorothy West is a writer of the period who has had a literary career spanning more that sixty years. Her novel *The Living Is Easy* was not published until 1948, and yet it reflects some of the basic thoughts of the Harlem Renaissance, with its focus on the strivings of Boston's Black middle class for "improvement." The novel should be considered important as it links together a tradition that runs from Frances Harper and Jessie Fauset to Paule Marshall and Alice Walker, yet West remains virtually unknown in the tradition of Afro-American writing, and in Afro-American women's writing as well.[21]

West and Johnson traveled the same circles during the Renaissance, but their interests took slightly different directions. For one thing, West preferred the route of independent publishing. After she returned to Boston, she founded and edited *Challenge: A Literary Quarterly*, in 1934. The magazine attracted the Renaissance talent, including a significant number of the women. Helene Johnson's poetry appeared in its premier issue. The magazine published once again in 1936, and lasted through two additional issues in 1935 and 1936 before it was reorganized with a new direction and a new associate editor, Richard Wright.[22] For many years, West wrote a regular column for the *Vineyard Gazette* (Martha's Vineyard, Massachusetts). Her short stories are currently being collected for publication, and a play based on her novel *The Living is Easy* is now being written.[23]

May Miller is the daughter of the distinguished scholar of sociology, Kelly Miller. Miller's popularity during the Renaissance period was due primarily to her acting and playwriting, which began while she was still a student at Howard University. Her award-winning plays were popular throughout the twenties and thirties. Her plays and poetry, published and unpublished, are in such sufficient quantity that it seems odd to consider her a "lost" artist, but today she is.[24] She collaborated with Willis Richardson to Publish *Negro History in Thirteen Plays* in 1935, which included four of her own plays, *Christophe's Daughters, Harriett Tubman, Samory,* and *Sojourner Truth.* In the mid-forties Miller's energies shifted to poetry, and she has since published seven volumes of poems. Lotus Press in Detroit is currently preparing an edition of her collected poems and plays.

In addition to those discussed above, other women writers of the period include Regina Anderson Andrews (1901–), Mae [Virginia] Cowdery (1903–1953), Blanch Taylor Dickinson (1896–?), and Lucy Ariel Williams Holloway (1905–). Anderson helped to organize the Harlem Experimental Theatre and had two of her plays performed there, *Climbing Jacob's Ladder,* 1925, and *Underground,* 1931. Dickinson didn't live in Harlem but she published in *Opportunity, Crisis,* and *Caroling Dusk,* as well as in newspapers in Kentucky, Illinois, and Pennsylvania.[25] Cowdery published *We Lift Our Voices and Other Poems* in 1936, and Williams, an Alabama native who studied and taught music, was for many years director of music at North Carolina Central University (Durham).

I have many memories associated with the women writers. I recall Lucy Ariel Williams's poem "Northboun," which won a prize in 1926 from *Opportunity* magazine. Her triumph was immensely pleasurable to me.[26] As for more personal reminiscences, I had the pleasure of meeting Gwendolyn Bennett, of visiting Anne Spencer in her garden, and even as a child, delighted in seeing Zora Neale Hurston in New Orleans. While I was not aware of it at the time, I am sure these women served as ready models as my own poetic imagination began to grow. That we have not looked into them any more that we have is another of those travesties in American literature.

Notes

1. Until the appearance of *Their Eyes Were Watching God* (Urbana: University of Illinois, 1977) and *I Love Myself when I Am Laughing* (Old Westbury, N.Y.: The Feminist Press, 1979), an anthology edited by Alice Walker, Hurston's work was out of print. These books and Robert E. Hemenway's biography *Zora Neale Hurston* (Urbana: University of Illinois Press, 1979) have made Hurston's contribution to literature available to the world of scholarship and to the general public.

2. For a discussion of Georgia Douglas Johnson, see Gloria T. Hull, *Color, Sex, and Poetry: Three Women Writers of the Harlem Renaissance* (Bloomington: Indiana University Press, 1987), pp. 155–211.

3. Georgia Douglas Johnson, "THe Heart of a Woman," reprinted from James Weldon Johnson, *The Book of Negro Poetry* (New York: Harcourt, Brace and Co,. 1931), pp. 181–2.

4. Hull, *Color, Sex, and Poetry*, p. 157.

5. Hull, *Color, Sex, and Poetry*, p. 161.

6. Hull, *Color, Sex, and Poetry*, pp. 172–3.

7. See *Give Us Each Day: The Diary of Alice Dunber-Nelson*, ed. Gloria T. Hull (New York: Norton, 1984), published for the first time after its discovery by Hull, and *Color, Sex, and Poetry*, pp. 33–104. All biographical information on Dunbar-Nelson is taken from *Color, Sex, and Poetry*, pp. 36, 49, 67–9.

8. Hull, *Color, Sex, and Poetry*, p. 77.

9. Sylvester Watkins, ed., *Anthology of American Negro Literature* (New York: Modern Library, 1944); William Stanley Braithwaite, ed., *Anthology of Magazine Verse, 1913–1929, and Yearbook of American Poetry* (annual) (New York: G. Sully, 1929); James Weldon Johnson, ed., *The Book of American Negro Poetry* (New York: Harcourt, Brace, 1922); Countee Cullen, ed., *Caroling Dusk: An Anthology of Verse by Negro Poets* (New York: Harper and Brothers, 1927); Sterling Brown, Arthur P. Davis, Ulysses Lee, eds., *The Negro Caravan* (1941) (New York: Arno Press, 1969); and Langston Hughes and Arna Bontemps, eds., *The Poetry of the Negro, 1746–1949: An Anthology* (Garden City, N.Y.: Doubleday, 1951). *Black Sister: Poetry by Black American Women, 1746–1980* (Bloomington: Indiana University Press, 1981), edited by Erlene Stetson, is the most recent and comprehensive source of women's writings of this period.

10. "Harlem: Mecca of the New Negro," a special issue of *Survey Graphic* 6, no. 6 (March 1925). Reprinted as *The New Negro* (n.d.). Poetry by Georgia Douglas Johnson, Helene Johnson, Gwendolyn Bennett, Angelina Grimké, and Anne Spencer is included here.

11. *Fire!!* appeared in a single issue in November 1926, edited by Wallace

Thurman, et al. Published during the height of the Renaissance, it reflected the radical ideas of the period both in theme and content. Gwendolyn Bennett and Helene Johnson both had poems in the issue. *Ebony and Topaz*, a special issue of *Opportunity*, edited by Charles S. Johnson, was published in 1927. *Ebony and Topaz* contained works by the major poets of the period as well as poems by Black student writers from Fisk, Howard, and Lincoln universities.

12. Spencer is anthologized in Johnson's *The Book of American Negro Poetry*, Locke's *The New Negro*, and Cullen's *Caroling Dusk*. Her poems first appeared in *The Crisis*, in 1920.

13. Johnson, p. 213.

14. Reprinted from Johnson, p. 18. J. Lee Greene's biography is the major source of information for Anne Spencer. See *Time's Unfading Garden: Anne Spencer's Life and Poetry* (Baton Rouge: Louisiana State University Press, 1977).

15. *Dictionary of Literary Biography* (DLB) 51, eds. Trudier Harris and Thadious M. Davis. (Detroit: Gale Research Co., 1987), pp. 3–51. A bibliography of Bennett's works is listed in the *DLB* 51 entry. A biographical work is currently being prepared by Sandra Y. Govan, who has written several essays on Bennett and who coauthored the *DLB* entry.

16. Charlemae Rollins includes Newsome in her *Famous American Negro Poets* (New York: Mead & Company, 1965), p. 57; *DLB* 51, pp. 126–9 is the biographical entry and contains a bibliography of her works.

17. The full title is *Gladiola Garden: Poems of Outdoors and Indoors for Second Grade Readers* (Washington, D.C.: Associated Publishers, 1940).

18. The most extensive discussion of Grimké's life and work is Hull's *Color, Sex, and Poetry*, pp. 107–55. Also see *DLB* 50, edited by Trudier Harris and Thadious M. Davis (Detroit: Gale Research Co. 1986), pp. 149–55.

19. Reprinted form Arnold Adoff, ed., *The Poetry of Black America* (New York: Harper & Row, 1973), p. 104.

20. *DLB* 51, p. 166. The Johnson entry appears on pages 164–7.

21. *The Living Is Easy* was reissued by The Feminist Press in 1982.

22. *New Challenge* was the second series, which began publishing in 1937 with a historic first issue that has since become a classic in Afro-American intellectual history. It contained Wright's famous "Blueprint for Negro Writing," and poetry by a new generation of socially conscious writers, most of whom were to become famous in the decades following. Langston Hughes, Sterling Brown, Frank Marshall, and Margaret Walker were among the writers represented.

23. Telephone conversation between Barbara Hunt (Afro-American Novel Project, University of Mississippi) and Dorothy West, November 17, 1988.

24. Three unpublished plays by Miller include "Stragglers in the Dust" (1930), "Nails and Thorns" (1933), and "Freedom's Children on the March" (1943). See *Dictionary of Literary Biography* 41, edited by Trudier Harris and Thadious M. Davis (Detroit: Gale Research Co., 1985), pp. 241–7.

25. Ann Allen Shockley, *Afro-American Women Writers 1746–1933: An Anthology and Critical Guide* (Boston: G. K. Hall, 1988), p. 450. Shockley's book offers brief commentaries on most of the women mentioned here, and is one of the few places where any information can be found on Anderson and Dickinson.

26. Williams did not publish a volume of poetry until some years after the Renaissance, *Shape Them into Dreams: Poems* (New York: Exposition, 1955), but her prize-winning poem brought her early prominence.

New Poets of the Forties and the Optimism of the Age

During the past twenty years of literary history in America—the 1930s and 1940s—Negroes have enjoyed unusual prominence as poets. At least ten books of poetry by new poets have received serious critical comment in leading literary magazines and columns. If we can believe the additional comments in anthologies of American poetry and books of literary criticism, Negroes writing poetry have gone a long way toward achieving full literary status as American writers; and they have thus attained a measure of integration into contemporary schools of literary thought.

A backward look into American life during these two decades should provide a reason for this literary development and resurgence. It must also accountably tell the background of such poetry, and at the same time provide a basis for predicting the future of poetry written by Negroes in America. Let us, therefore, consider, first, the socio-economic and political factors that have influenced the poetry of the past twenty years.

During the twenties, we spoke of the "New Negro" and the Negro Renaissance. At that time such figures as James Weldon Johnson (1871–1938), Langston Hughes (1902–67), Countee Cullen (1903–46), Claude McKay (1889–1948), and Jean Toomer (1894–1967) emerged as the

This essay was first published under the title "New Poets" in *Phylon* 11, no. 4 (1950): 345–54. Reprinted by permission.

spokesmen of the New Negro. Rich white patrons or "angels," who could and did underwrite the poetry of Negroes by supporting Negroes, did so as a fad to amuse themselves and their guests at some of their fabulous parties. They considered the intelligent, sensitive, and creative Negro as the "talented tenth"—an exotic, bizarre, and unusual member of his race—and they indulgently regarded the poetry of the Negro as the prattle of a gifted child. Negro people as a mass showed little appreciation for poetry and offered very little audience for the Negro writing poetry. Whatever Negro people thought about the poetry written about Negro life did not seem to matter. In the final analysis, the audience and the significant critics were white. Negroes as a whole knew too little about their own life to analyze correctly and judge astutely their own literary progress as poets. Isolated from the literary life of whites and confused by the segregated pattern of economic and political life, these writers lacked social perspective and suffered from a kind of literary myopia. Poets of the Harlem Renaissance seemed constantly to beg the question of the Negro's humanity, perhaps as an answer to the white patron's attitude that Negroes were only children anyway.

The twenties saw *God's Trombones* (1927) by James Weldon Johnson, *The Weary Blues* (1926) by Langston Hughes, *Color* (1925) and *Copper Sun* (1927) by Countee Cullen, and *Harlem Shadows* (1922) by Claude McKay. Each collection was received as justification that the Negro race could produce geniuses and that it was nothing short of remarkable that "God should make a poet Black and bid him sing." Titles of books as well as such eloquent short lyrics as "O Black and Unknown Bards," "I, too, Sing America," and "I Am the Darker Brother," all reflect an intense desire to justify the Negro as a human being. These books sold well among whites, but none of them ranked as bestsellers. Most people did not buy poetry, certainly not poetry by Negroes. It was a day of individual literary patronage, when a rich "angel" adopted a struggling poor artist and made an exotic plaything out of any "really brilliant Negro."

The halcyon days of individual patronage of the arts ended with the stockmarket crash. The gay hayride of the flaming and gilded twenties came to a jolting stop, and the depression of the thirties began to make its first inroads into American life. Hoover persisted so long in predicting that prosperity was just around the corner that it became a standing joke. Evictions were common and communism was on the march. What chance did the luxury of art have at such a time?

Roosevelt's New Deal not only averted a bloody social revolution in 1932 and 1933 by bracing the tottering economic structure of the country, but it

also ushered into existence a boon to art and letters in the form of the Works
Progress Administration. The WPA meant two things of far-reaching significance to Negro writers. It meant, first (as it meant to whites), money on
which to exist and provision for the meager security necessary in order to
create art. It meant, second, that Negroes who were creative writers, and
poets especially, were no longer entirely isolated from whites. In cities above
the Mason-Dixon Line where the writers' projects drew no color lines, a new
school of Black and white writers mushroomed into being overnight.

The cry of these writers was the cry of social protest: protest against the
social ills of the day, including unemployment, slums, crime, juvenile
delinquency, prejudice, poverty, and disease. The New Deal struggled to
alleviate these social ills, while the writers led the vanguard of literary protest
and agitation for a better world. Negro poets joined the ranks of these socially
conscious writers and Negroes who were writing poetry in particular were
poets of social protest.

At least three new poets appeared during the 1930s, with books of poetry
of obvious social significance. *Southern Road* by Sterling Brown appeared in
1932. It was chiefly concerned with the plight of Negroes in the South.
Ballads in this volume such as the Slim Greer series are some of the finest in
the annals of both Negro and white American poetry. One of Brown's later
poems, "Old Lem," which first appeared in magazines and anthologies in
the thirties, is an outstanding example of social protest and clearly reflects the
mood of the period.

> I talked to old Lem
> And old Lem said:
> "They weigh the cotton
> They store the corn
>   We only good enough
>   To work the rows;
> They run the commissary
> They keep the books
>   We gotta be grateful
> For being cheated;
> Whippersnapper clerks
> Call us out of our name
>   We got to say mister
>   To spindling boys
> They make our figgers
> Turn somersets
>   We buck in the middle

Say, "Thankyuh, sah."
They don't come by ones
They don't come by twos
But they come by tens.[1]

Black Man's Verse, and *I Am the American Negro,* by Grank Marshall Davis appeared in 1935, and 1937 respectively. These two volumes of poetry, although technically rough and uneven, are scathing books of social protest. For example, in "Portrait of the Cotton South," Davis writes,

Well, you remakers of America
You apostles of Social Change
Here is pregnant soil

Here are grass roots of a nation.
But the crop they grow is Hate and Poverty.
By themselves they will make no change
Black men lack the guts
Po' whites have not the brains
And the big land owners want Things as They Are[2]

Black Labor Chant by David Wadsworth Cannon, who died before his volume of verse was published in 1939, celebrated the Negro's joining ranks with the upsurging Labor movement, particularly the CIO, and continued in general in the vein of social protest.

Although the outbreak of the Second World War changed the note of social significance, bringing as it did prosperity at home in the United States, and ushering into the world the Atomic Age, the strong note of anxiety it bred was not felt at first in the literature of the period. For at least a decade longer the poetry of American Negroes continued to reflect the mood of the thirties. A half-dozen books of poetry published during the forties reflect either a note of social protest or a growing concern with the terrible reality of war. *Heart-Shape in the Dust* by Robert Hayden appeared in 1940, followed by my own volume *For My People,* in 1942. *Rendezvous with America* by Melvin Tolson was published in 1944; *A Street in Bronzeville* by Gwendolyn Brooks was published in 1945; and *Powerful Long Ladder* by Owen Dodson appeared in 1946. The first three poets each reflected in varying degrees the note of social protest expressed in the preceding decade. The last two poets, however, showed a growing concern with the grim realities of war.

Heart-Shape in the Dust by Robert Hayden appeared in 1940, followed by my own volume *For My People,* in 1942. *Rendezvous with America* by Melvin Tolson was published in 1944; *A Street in Bronzeville* by Gwendolyn

Brooks was published in 1945; and *Powerful Long Ladder* by Owen Dodson
appeared in 1946. The first three poets each reflected in varying degrees the
note of social protest expressed in the preceding decade. The last two poets,
however, showed a growing concern with the grim realities of war.

From Robert Hayden's early work *Heart-Shape in the Dust*, an excerpt
from the poem "Speech" follows:

Hear me, white brothers,
Black brothers, hear me:

I have seen the hand
Holding the blowtorch
To the dark, anguish-twisted body;
I have seen the hand
Giving the high-sign
To fire on the white pickets;
And it was the same hand,
Brothers, listen to me,
It was the same hand.[3]

From my own poem, "For My People:"

For my people standing staring trying to fashion a
better way from confusion, from hypocrisy and misunder-
standing, trying to fashion a world that will hold all the people, all
the faces, all the adams and eves and
their countless generations;
Let a new earth rise. Let another world be born.
Let a bloody peace be written in the sky. Let a second
generation full of courage issue forth; let a people
loving freedom come to growth. Let a beauty full of
healing and a strength of final clenching be the
pulsing in our spirits and our blood. Let the martial
songs be written, let the dirges disappear. Let a race
of men now rise and take control.[4]

From Melvin Tolson's poem, "Dark Symphony":

Out of abysses of Illiteracy,
Through labyrinths of Lies,
Across the waste lands of Disease . . .

We advance!
Out of dead-ends of Poverty,
Through wildernesses of Superstition,
Across barricades of Jim Crowism . . .
We advance!

With the Peoples of the World . . .
We advance![5]

The poems of Gwendolyn Brooks and Owen Dodson reflect a growing concern with the problems of war. They show, more than any of the aforementioned poets, the growing global perspective that has become a keynote of current poetry.

In her volume *A Street in Bronzeville* Brooks writes about "Gay Chaps at the Bar":

We know how to order . . .
But nothing ever taught us to be islands.
. . . . No stout
Lesson showed how to chat with death. We brought
No brass fortissimo, among our talents,
To holler down the lions in this air.[6]

In Owen Dodson's poems "Black Mother Praying" and "Conversation on V," the question of race is presented within the framework of war. The following excerpt is taken from "Conversation on V":

V stands for Victory.
Now what is this here Victory?
It what we get when we fight for it.
Ought to be Freedom, God do know that.[7]

The period of greatest intensification of the social note in poetry written by Negroes extends roughly from 1935 to 1945. During this time, the New Negro came of age. He rejected the status of the exotic, the accidentally unusual, the talented tenth of what the white audience chose to consider an otherwise mentally infantile minority group whose masses were illiterate, disfranchised, exploited, and oppressed. Negroes became members of a new school of writers who were no longer isolated because of color, who were integrated around the beliefs that created the New Deal. They were the poets of social protest who began to catch a glimmer of a global perspective, who, as speakers for their race, did not beg the question of their humanity, and who cried out to other peoples over the earth to recognize race prejudice as a weapon that is as dangerous as the atomic bomb in the threat to annihilation of culture and peace in the western world.

Any literary development of the Negro in the thirties was directly due to his social development. During the thirties the Negro people made great social strides. The New Deal opened many avenues of opportunity and development to the masses of Negro people. The economic standards of the Negro race rose higher than ever in the history of his life in this country. As a result of free art for all the people a cultural renaissance in all the arts swept the United States. This created a new intelligentsia with a genuine appreciation for the creative arts and a recognition for all cultural values. Labor was stimulated by the unionization together of Black and white labor and this in turn strengthened the political voice of the people. Consequently the literary audience widened and the Negro people themselves grew in intellectual awareness.

The distinguishing characteristics of the poetry of the 1940s can be most clearly seen in three books published during the forties: *From the Shaken Tower* by Bruce McMarion Wright, published in Great Britain in 1944; *The Lion and the Archer* by Robert Hayden, published as a brochure in 1948; and Gwendolyn Brooks's Pulitzer Prize-winning volume *Annie Allen*, published in 1949. All show a marked departure from the note of social protest. Each one of these books is less preoccupied with the theme of race as such. Race is rather used as a point of departure toward a global point of view. The tendency is toward internationalism rather than nationalism and racism. Because modern inventions have shortened the time involved in transportation and communications to such an amazing degree, our world has shrunk to a small community of nations and mankind is forced to recognize the kinship of all peoples. Thus we have a basis for new conceptions that of necessity lead us in new directions.

These new poets of the late forties also remind us that there are other factors in the writing of poetry that are equally as important as perspective. They focus our attention on craftsmanship with an emphasis on form. Their poetry has universal appeal coupled with this return to form. These poets show an emphasis on technique rather than on subject matter, and a moving toward intellectual themes of psychological implications that often border on obscurantism. These poems are never primitive, simple, and commonplace.

What technical advances have these poets of our new classical age shown over the poets of the twenties and thirties? Looking back to the twenties one quickly recognizes that the poets of the Negro Renaissance varied technically from the strictly classical and conventional poetry to the utterly unconventional. Countee Cullen was an outstanding example of the true classicist who had been schooled thoroughly in versification and in all the types and forms of poetry. His classical education was clearly reflected in his poetry. On the other hand, Langston Hughes introduced the pattern of the "blues" into poetry. He made no pretense of being the poet's poet, of writing intellectual poetry, or conforming to any particular school of aesthetics. The pattern of the "blues" was, nevertheless, the first new Negro idiom introduced into American poetry since the time of Paul Laurence Dunbar (1872–1906), whose Negro dialect poetry was typical of the antebellum plantation life. The poetry of Negroes that was published during the thirties was primarily free verse. Technically there were no innovations.

Currently, however, the new poets are so concerned with form that they often exclude everything else and thus are in danger of sacrificing sense for sound, or meaning for music. As a result of this tendency, poetry by white writers in America has been labeled obscurantist. Can this charge be safely leveled at recent poetry by Negroes?

Such a charge was leveled at *Annie Allen* when the book was reviewed in *Phylon*. The poem "the birth in a narrow room" was said to have too many elliptical or truncated lines. This seems a minor technical matter, since the technique does not destroy the meaning of the poem. The criticized lines follow:

Weeps out of western country something new.
Blurred and stupendous. Wanted and unplanned.
   Winks. Twines, and weakly winks
Upon the milk-glass fruit bowl, iron pot,
The bashful china child tipping forever
Yellow apron and spilling pretty cherries. [8]

Does this make sense? Obviously when one reads the entire poem in terms of the title, the poem does make sense, and that should be all that really matters.

The fact that Brooks displays an excellent knowledge of form, whether in the versatile handling of types of forms of poetry included in *Annie Allen* or in the metrical variations in the volume, can be readily seen as proof of this new emphasis upon conventional form. She skillfully handles a number of stanzaic forms including couplets, quatrains, the Italian terza rima, and even in "The Anniad," the difficult rhyme royal or the seven-line stanza named for Chaucer. Here is a perfect example:

Think of thaumaturgic lass
Looking in her looking-glass
At the unembroidered brown;
Printing bastard roses there;
Then emotionally aware
Of the black and boisterous hair
Taming all that anger down.[9]

Annie Allen also includes several poems written in free verse as well as occasional lines of blank verse, short lyrics, ballads, and sonnets. The volume is a tour de force of poetic virtuosity.

Thematically *Annie Allen* is a fine delineation of the character of a young Negro woman from childhood through adolescence to complete maturity, but except for slight details of race, the portrait could apply to any female in a certain class or society. The entire volume, shot through with a highly sophisticated humor, is not only technically certain, but also vindicates the promise of *A Street in Bronzeville.* Coming after the long complaint of white critics that Negro poets lack form and intellectual acumen, Brooks's careful craftsmanship and sensitive understanding, reflected in *Annie Allen*, are not only personal triumphs but a racial vindication.

There may be more reason to level the charge of obscurantism at the poetry of Myron O'Higgins in *The Lion and the Archer*, a collection containing poems by O'Higgins and poems by Robert Hayden. Although the vocabulary is no more intellectual than that of Brooks, and although there are several magnificent poems in this brochure, there seems to be more obscurity and ambiguity in O'Higgins use of poetic symbols and imagery, as for example in:

But that day in between
comes back with two lean cats
who run in checkered terror
through a poolroom door
and bolting from a scream
a keen knife marks with sudden red
the gaming green
. . . a purple billiard hall
explodes the color scheme.[10]

Robert Hayden, on the other hand, shows a decided growth and advance in this volume over his first, *Heart-Shape in the Dust*, which was uneven and lacked the grasp of a true Negro idiom, which he seemed to be seeking at that time. His sense of choric movement and his understanding and perspective of peoples have increased to a telling degree and he writes now with due maturity and power:

Now as skin-and-bones Europe burst all over from the swastika's
hexentanz: oh think of Anton, Anton brittle, Anton crystalline;
think what the winter moon, the leper beauty of a Gothic tale, must see:
the ice-azure likeness of a young man reading, carved most craftily.[11]

In Bruce McWright there is authentic reporting of World War II, but even the title of his book, *From the Shaken Tower*, reflects the questions of our present age. War has further denounced the ivory towers, because war is the grim reality that ends the romantic dreams and airy castle building. The poets of the thirties said that ivory towers were not fit habitations for poets anyway; they should be social prophets, preachers, teachers, and leaders. With the threat of annihilation hanging over the civilized world of western culture, whether by the atomic or hydrogen bomb, with the tremendous wave of social revolution sweeping through the world, men have felt themselves spiritually bankrupt. There is, therefore, a wave of religious revival, especially in America, whether through fear and hysteria or from a genuine desire for self-analysis, reflection and introspective knowledge that may lead, thereby, to a spiritual panacea that we seek for the ills of the world. Whether it is Catholicism, existentialism, or communism, modern man is turning to some definite belief around which to integrate his life and give it true wholeness and meaning. Consequently there has already been noted among white writers a decided religious revival. Whereas Marxism was the intellectual fad at present in America, where the political and economic structures have definitely reverted to an extremely conservative position. The religious pathway of T. S. Eliot, prophet of the spiritual wasteland, technical pioneer, and most influential name among poets during the thirties, had been followed by W. H. Auden. Robert Lowell, a Pulitzer Prize poet, is a Catholic convert. Thus far no Negro recently writing poetry has reflected this religious revival, but we may well expect this tendency.

Negroes not only have grown up as poets technically, with volumes of poetry showing a growing concern with craftsmanship, social perspective, and intellectual maturity, but they have also begun to reap the rewards in the form of laurels due them for their labors. They have received a greater measure of consideration from literary critics and judges of literary competitions than ever before in the history of writing by Negroes in America. Not only have Negroes succeeded in winning many philanthropic grants, such as Rosenwalds and Guggenheims, which have provided the wherewithal to pursue creative projects and develop burgeoning talents, but also many other honors and awards have been granted to poets of the Negro race. These have included grants from the Academy of Arts and Letters and a Yale award for a promising younger poet. Now in 1950 has come the signal achievement of the Pulitzer Prize to Gwendolyn Brooks for *Annie Allen*. This is the first time in the history of this prize that a Negro has won this national honor.[2] With this announcement comes not only the recognition of the fact that poetry by Negroes has come of age, but also that the Negro has finally achieved full status in the literary world as an American poet.

What, then is the future of the Negro writing poetry in America? It would seem from these that the outlook is bright and hopeful. It is a fact that some of the most significant poetry written in America during the past decades has been written by Negroes. Now, what is the promise? Is there hope that it will be fulfilled? Is the Negro as a poet doomed to annihilation because he is part of a doomed western world, or is that western culture really doomed? Is our society already a fascist society? If it is, what hope has our literature? If these are only bogeymen, then whither are we turning? Is our path toward religious revival, neoclassicism, internationalism a result of global perspectives and world government, or what?

If we are truly in a transitional stage of social evolution, a state of flux, of cataclysmic socioeconomic and political upheaval that will ultimately and inevitably shape our literary life, this will soon be clear. Now, the shape of our emerging society is dimly shadowed by many imponderables. The future of the Negro writing poetry in America is bright only if the future of the world is bright and if we with the rest of our world can survive the deadly conflicts that threaten us and our total freedom, the awful anticipation of which now hangs over our heads like the sword of Damocles.

Notes

1. Sterling A. Brown, *The Complete Poems of Sterling A. Brown*, ed. Michael S. Harper (New York: Harper & Row, 1980), p. 180.

2. Frank Marshall Davis, *47th Street* (Prairie City, Ill.: The Decker City Press, 1948), p. 38.

3. Robert Hayden, *Heart-Shape in the Dust* (Detroit: Falcon Press, 1940), p. 27.

4. Margaret Walker, *For My People* (New Haven, Conn.: Yale University Press, copyright 1942, seventh printing, 1969), p. 14.

5. Melvin B. Tolson, *Rendezvous with America* (New York: Dodd, Mead & Company, 1944), pp. 41–2.

6. Gwendolyn Brooks, *The World of Gwendolyn Brooks* (New York: Harper & Row, 1971), p. 48.

7. Owen Dodson, *Powerful Long Ladder* (1946; reprinted, New York: Farrar, Straus & Giroux, 1970), p. 91.

8. Brooks, *The World of Gwendolyn Brooks*, p. 67.

9. Ibid., p. 84.

10. Myron O'Higgins, "Two Lean Cats," *The Lion and the Archer* (Nashville, Tenn.: Hemphill Press, 1949), p. 12.

11. Robert Hayden, "Eine Kleine Nachtmusik," *The Lion and the Archer*, p. 6.

12. Walker wrote this essay before the Pulitzer Prizes had been awarded to Alice Walker and Toni Morrison and the Nobel Prize to African playwright Wale Soyinka.

Some Aspects of the Black Aesthetic

During its years of existence, the Institute for the Study of History, Life, and Culture of Black People at Jackson State University has sponsored exhibitions of graphic and plastic art by Black artists from Africa, the Caribbean, and Black America. These have included a collection of African sculpture owned by Doris Derby, an exhibition of prints by Margaret Burroughs, paintings and prints by Rosalind Jeffries, Jewel Simon, John Biggers, Skunder Boghassian, Lois Mailou Jones (Mrs. Pierre-Noel), Jeff Donaldson, Charles White, Elizabeth Catlett, Harold Dorsey, and a group of Haitian painters. We have had such exhibitions of sculpture, prints, and paintings despite the handicap of having no formal gallery.

These artists have of necessity been exponents of various artistic schools, of varying political and philosophic viewpoints, and are from many different geographical locations. Although they share an African heritage, they do not of necessity share the same ideology nor see the functions and values of their artistic productions in the same way. And despite our earnest efforts to educate our students and community with an appreciation for, and history of, art by Black people, we have in no way attempted to foist upon them our own social and political beliefs, nor have we wanted artists to proselytize

This essay originally appeared in *Freedomways* 16, no. 2 (1976): 95–102. Reprinted by permission.

them nor in turn be proselytized. Nevertheless, it would be foolhardy to suggest that we at the Institute believe in art for art's sake. This, to me, seems a direct contradiction of all the humanistic traditions of Afro-American art and literature. The gospel of social justice, freedom, peace, and human dignity has been preached in all the art of Afro-America from its beginnings to the present. The slogan "Art for the People" is not a new nor radically different tag from what it has always been among Black people. African art from its ancient beginnings has always been functional in its highest spiritual sense. Art and artifacts were created with deep religious and sexual meaning, and whether ceremonial or functional, were therefore sacred.

At the present time our cultural expression is threatened by anti-humanistic forces. In a technological universe undergoing radical and cataclysmic social change and in a transitional period from the old economic and political order of western capitalism and financial imperialism to a new world of peoples' humanism, cultural pluralism, and socialism (if hopefully, in truth, that is our direction) we must pause. Those of us who are custodians and creators of a truly Black heritage of creativity and who are daily producing our cultural wares that are authentic expressions of the Black experience in all of us whose business it is to hammer out art in the Black fires of our own imaginations—we are called upon to make real and various decisions, to discover new departures, and to give our talented world-youth new directions, or reassess old directions, in the light of new developments.

A time bomb is ticking away at our lives. A new age is converging upon us. It is time our thinking Black world became a whirling world of action. The entire Republican syndrome has been a social, political, economic, and cultural setback for Black people. We have suffered repression, reprisal, and gross neglect on the part of our national government, though I am sure that neglect has been more malign neglect than benign. The entire twentieth century of war and revolution is only one factor in understanding what is happening on the continent of Africa. Likewise, the crises of world leadership, war and peace, money, food, and the lack of cheap, safe, nuclear energy for a nuclear age—all these factors are the stuff out of which great art is produced.

Years ago, in New Orleans, I began to preach the doctrine I am using as my text today. At that time I said we Black people must use our art, music, literature, history, and religious expression as foundations for a new educational system, because American education as founded on Newtonian physics is obsolete. The Einsteinian revolution at the beginning of this century gave man a new concept of the universe: illimitable with a spacetime continuum, and demanding unity in diversity, demanding the maintaining of our ethnicity and racial identity, our culture in a world of cultural pluralism. Years ago, in Chicago, at the Black Academy, we talked about an Agenda for Artistic Action in the decade of the seventies—a decade like the fifties and more and more demanding that we support our mushrooming young Black artists: painters, poets, actors, musicians, rising in a half-dozen or more cultural centers all over these United States. These centers range from John O. Killens's writers' workshops in Harlem, Brooklyn, at Columbia, Howard, and Fisk; to the Watts writers' workshop in California; the Organization of Black American Culture in Chicago; and the Free Southern Theater in Jackson and New Orleans; and other similar centers in Newark, Atlanta, and Birmingham. In two articles written during 1975 on the subject of Black culture, I have further indicated the directions that I believe we should be taking.[1] Obviously, I believe that our art should always be an expression of our lives, should be more than an expression of our Black world—it is always a cultural tool toward the unity of that Black world and further toward a world understanding not only of our Black humanity but of common humanity.

Today, in the exigencies of an uncertain present and a more turbulent future, we must constantly ask ourselves what we are doing to build that culturally free tomorrow for our children; what we have been about, what we are about, what we ought to be about.

What is it we Black artists have in common, whether we are poets, musicians, actors, painters, sculptors, or architects? A small beginning has been made toward a written body of aesthetics for Black artists. There is much work to be done. James Porter, and others have begun this "Bible" in painting; Alain Locke, Sterling Brown, Larry Neal, and others in literature; and Eileen Southern, along with Maude Cuney Hare, in music.

Is there a "Black" aesthetic? A number of my scholarly Black friends in academic circles with degrees from white American universities have said, "Now Margaret, you know there is no such animal!" And yet these very Black scholars have made real contributions to a aesthetic of Afro-American literature. Certainly I learned no such doctrine from my white professors at Northwestern, Yale, or Iowa, and in the annals of Anglo-Saxon and Anglo-American literature, no such creature exists. What then do we mean by a "Black aesthetic"? What do we mean by aesthetics or any general aesthetic? Webster's definition, though far too limited in scope, makes a beginning: "That branch of philosophy dealing with the beautiful, chiefly with respect to theories of its essential character, tests by which it may be judged, and its relation to the human mind; also the branch of psychology treating of the sensations and emotions evoked by the fine arts and 'belles lettres.'" This further involves principles of beauty and good taste in terms of this fine art.

The methods for imitating, creating or recreating nature all go back to primitive cultures, just as the beginnings of religion or medicine grow out of superstitious beliefs and fears, and out of magic and witchcraft. All of this began in our ancient motherland of Africa. The earliest theory of inspiration, for example, grows out of the symbol behind the Greek and Latin word *inspirate*, or to breathe in, or inhale the smoke, the air, the dust, the spirits (for the spirits inhabit all of these) and, likewise, to exhale in oracular tones or predictions those same spirits in the dust, in the smoke, in the fire, in the water. Second, in the strange orphic rites of the mysteries surrounding birth, puberty, courtship, marriage, reproduction, childbirth, and death may be understood the parallel process of conception, organization, and realization. Third, and finally, spell possession and exorcism or control over the spell and the destruction or overpowering of demons or devils are explanations for creative inspiration; they are, in short, imagination.[2]

I tell my students that imagination is nothing more than the recurrence, over and over, of an image or picture perceived, or the repetition in the brain of a concept so conceived as the beginning of idea. Creative thinking is therefore both perceptive and apperceptive, or conceptual. The creative process therefore begins with this creative thinking. Concepts or mental images like perceptions or transferred physical pictures by means of the sensory stimuli are really the beginnings of thought and, in turn, of ideas. Written words, we know, are merely symbols of and for these concepts or perceptions. Communication is possible only between those speaking the same language, or understanding the same symbols. Figurative language is therefore the tool of the poet. Figurations and configurations of concepts, thoughts, and ideas are the keys to the inner thinking of the creative artist or thinker. If one is a musician, the concept will be translated, or transformed, into a musical motif as the initial unit of his composition. If one is a painter, one must translate conceptualization into color, line, movement, or form within a given space, or spatial limitations. If one is an architect, again one addresses oneself to a certain use of space with design further acting as medium and mechanism of control.

The poet uses figurative language of metaphor and simile to combine image, rhythm, and meaning in a whole composition, seeking thereby to express a concept or vision or perception of truth and beauty. And always these are determined within the frame of reference of experience or observation, as the artist both conceives and perceives the world outside and the world within.

Now, let us consider the development of such a system from the standpoint of the Black artist. This, it seems, necessitates some historical recapitulation and, second, involves an analytical study of the products or works of Black artists in any given school or national body of work and, third, involves standards of judgment in terms of "Beauty" according to form and content. When we consider beauty and truth, wholeness and proportion, the dynamics of space and form, color, line, and movement, tension and conflict, is there any standard that is not universal, raceless and nonnationalistic? If all temperaments were the same, there would be no such need, and if all persons used the same standards, there would be no further need but, alas, this is not true. Whether good or bad, there are relative standards of physical beauty, there are racial and national concepts of both space and time, and differing standards of taste and judgment that determine any people's art and criticism. And just as there are Anglo-Saxon and white American standards by virtue of our inequitable systems of education, religious institutions, and separated ethnic and national cultures there are, of necessity, a Black standard, a set of Black value judgments, and what is more, a history of traditions of Black idioms and Black conceptualizations that determine this ethos and this philosophic system of aesthetics. This we propose to show as a Black aesthetic—indigenous to Black people, having its roots in ancient Black Africa and characterized by certain marked traits seen throughout the diaspora in the modern Black world. Furthermore, if we may be so bold as to declare it, this system is basic to all other systems. Like all world religions, cultural expressions of art, music, literature, and language, this ancient Black African system is the oriental foundation for all occidental systems that have grown out of it.

To understand such a Black aesthetic it is necessary to study ancient Africa and observe closely Egyptian architecture, religions, culture, coffin texts, and the Book of the Dead. African language of the drum and plastic arts, and the cave drawings of Tassili before the days of the Sahara Desert reflect the long and respected cultural ideas of the "Cradle of Mankind." This ancient civilization predates Greece and Rome and even the Semitic influence of the fertile crescent. This is a culture that these neighboring and developing cultures in their earliest explorations found already in a highly advanced state in Egypt and that existed nearly 3,500 years before Christ. Only in Sumer was there an older culture.

What then do we Black artists have in common as principals in this Black aesthetic? What is our heritage from ancient Africa—whether we are painters and sculptors, musicians, architects, poets, prophets, or priests? What is the common system that we share—whether we are Afro-Americans, Afro-Caribbeans, or native Black Africans? Is it first and foremost our gift of creativity, our standards of the human body, and realistic portrayals of our conceptions of nature, humans, and God? Is it only the great welter of tribal and folk belief? Is it the African sense of moral order, time, and social justice that we share? The Black idiom in our speech, art, religion, and communal living? Whatever you may understand it to mean, look for the evidences in West African sculpture, North African architecture in Egypt and Ethiopia, East African language and painting, and South African ritualistic literature.

When you have definitely and irrefutably discovered the sources and evidences of this Black idiom and Black aesthetic, observe their influences in the modern world, notably the influences of West African sculpture from the Nok, the Benin, the Ife, and the Ashanti peoples on the impressionistic, cubistic, and futuristic painting and sculpture of white Europeans, particularly Picasso, Brancusi, and Modigliani. Trace the native Black African rhythms to the flamenco music of Andalusia, the calypso music of the Caribbean, and the syncopated rhythms of American Negro jazz, blues, work songs, prison hollers, and the pathos of the spirituals. Look into the modern dances of the limbo and the hustle, the bump, the hucklebuck, the big apple, Charleston, cakewalk, shimmy, the boogie-woogie, Black-bottom, trucking, and jitterbugging in general. And, finally, if you search diligently through the speech of the people of the Sea Islands of Georgia—known familiarly as geechee, or through the Gullah of South Carolina, or even the patois of the Louisiana Black creole, you will find that Black African idiom. It is surely in all southern cooking, and above all, it is most apparent in the shout songs of our Black unorthodox churches and the cultic rituals of funerals, weddings, and vestiges of initiation or rites of passage from childhood to adolescence.

The Black aesthetic derives its standards of beauty, order, and cultural dynamism from these folk patterns of behavior and living—this welter of Black life, these Black idioms that are as ancient as our Black culture, which is as old as the Nile.

The Black artist distills art from life and Black art, therefore, is only a product of the Black aesthetic if it is an authentic expression of the Black experience. We do have an indigenous culture that has grown out of our ancient heritage, and this culture with its Black idiom, Black standard of beauty, Black truth of life and nature, forms a rich basis for a Black aesthetic.

For more than 350 years Afro-Americans have created a distinctive, humanistic, and culturally indigenous art in this country. Despite centuries of racial persecution and hardship, repression, violent intimidation, and reprisal, we have maintained an artistic expression that is physically and culturally tied to Black Africa in idiom, folk meaning, and authentic Black experience. This art has an emotive content, a human representational nature, and a stylized abstraction that is typical of the Black cultural dynamism descended from Africa. Yet it has, too, all the affective characteristics of our American environment and social struggle. It is time to make some hard decisions—to regroup as a result of our political setbacks and to reaffirm our national and cultural entities and assets. To understand and reclaim our ancient African past as heritage—to acknowledge our American nationhood as our new horizon—these are first steps toward our great future and spiritual destiny in a world of the twenty-first century, which we are building for our children.

Notes

1. "Interview with Margaret Walker Alexander and Charles H. Rowell." *Black World* 25 (1975): 4–17; and Margaret Walker Alexander, "A Poetic Equation: Conversation between Nikki Giovanni and Margaret Walker." *Negro History Bulletin* 38 (1975): 228. The latter essay was published in book form by Howard University Press in 1974.

2. Among useful sources for a further discussion of these ideas are: Gabriel Welch, *Africa Before They Came* (New York: William Morrow, 1965) and the works of Africanist Melville Herskovits, e.g., *Dahomean Narrative* (Evanston, Ill.: Northwestern University Press, 1958).

The Humanistic Tradition of Afro-American Literature

The literature of Black people in America is not a recent phenomenon. It is not a result of the recent interest in Black studies, although that recent interest has brought the large body of Afro-American literature to the attention of all Americans. A current issue of *Time* magazine devoted to Black America contains articles about Black people written largely by white staff members who know almost nothing about their subject. A white staff member confided to me that he knew the names of fewer than six Black writers; that he did not know whether Richard Wright was Black or white; he was familiar with two or three poets—Paul Laurence Dunbar, Langston Hughes, and Countee Cullen; and his assignment was to reveal a whole new world of Black literature. He asked me whether this literature had all been written in the past century, and he seemed dumbfounded to know that Black people have been creating and publishing a body of literature in this country since colonial days. What he did not stop long enough to learn was that the tradition of Afro-American literature began in the ancient oriental world; in Black Africa, in Egypt some thirty-five hundred years ago with the coffin texts and pyramids and the Book of the Dead. The literature of Black people, like that of all people, grew out of the cosmogony and cosmology that

An earlier version of this essay appeared in *American Libraries* (October 1970): 849–54. Reprinted with permission of the American Library Association. © 1970 by ALA.

developed around the Nile River and not from Greece or Rome at the end of the ancient world, nor from the Middle Ages and the European Renaissance (that grew out of the Renaissance already dead in Asia and Africa), nor with the modern expansion of European man. It is quite true that Afro-Americans have been thrice cut off from this oriental, African, ancient tradition: once by the Roman Empire, which became the transfer agent of the Ancient Orient to the Medieval Occident; again in the Middle Ages when the Christian Church, moving westward, left Africa and Asia to the spreading religion of Islam; and once again when Africa was pillaged by the slavers and colonized by the empires of Europe. We lost our religion, our language, and our other cultural ties of art, music, and the oral tradition of literature.

Despite this loss and despite laws forbidding education for Blacks, Black people learned the English language, and early in the eighteenth century, were writing and publishing this writing in the new world. Further, it is true that despite the fact that Afro-American literature reveals similar intellectual trends and technical devices in comparable periods, schools, and writers, and is basically American in language and form, it is totally different in tone and subject matter from that of white America. It is suffused with an emotive content that is humanistic, realistic, and historically tied in tradition to that ancient, oriental world of literature. It is still tied to Black Africa and to everything racially indigenous to Black people and nonwhite cultures everywhere in the world. This is the literature of an oppressed people; yet it is entirely different in emotive content from the literature of persecuted Jewish people. Nationalistically it is distinctly different from any national body of European literature. It may sometimes be of necessity Anglo-Saxon or Anglo-American in form, but never in content, in tone, or in philosophy; and always it is permeated with ideas of revolt against artifice, sterility, self-consciousness, contrived morality, and pseudonatural ethics. Whenever one sees this Black idiom at work in Afro-American literature, as in all artistic expression by Black people, it is antimoralistic, in the moralistic puritanical sense, antiformalistic, and antirationalistic. It demands a certain verve, what Arna Bontemps calls a certain "riff"; and above all, at its best it reflects the ultimate of the Black experience, or the life of Black people, in America: a people oppressed who refuse to be suppressed; a people who refuse to be dehumanized or made into machines, who refuse to give up their ancient inheritance of secular play, warmth, and gaiety of love and joy, or a continual awareness of the deepest spiritual meanings for freedom, peace, and human dignity; a people who have had to develop compassion out of suffering and who are passionately tied to all that is earthy, natural, and emotionally free.

It is, therefore, a strange phenomenon, but nevertheless quite true, that wherever Black Africans have lived as slaves or free men in Europe, South America, and North America they have carried with them from Black Africa great gifts with which to enrich any foreign land and culture they have known. For example, it is well known today that the rhythms of Africa have influenced the music of the modern world and that many musical instruments have their origin in ancient Black Africa. Black slaves and their descendants in America have left an indelible musical mark on America with blues, spirituals, work songs, jazz, and gospel music. African sculpture from the Benin, Ashanti, and Ife has influenced the modern art of Picasso, Modigliani, Brancusi, and others. This Black African influence is also seen in the folk literature of Black Americans, particularly in the folk heroes and the tall tales. This is a natural part of Afro-American literature despite centuries of cultural estrangement. To what extent the African religion of animism and the worship of the Loa, as Black slaves carried their Vodu, or gods, with them to foreign lands, affected and still affects the religion of Black Americans, both in orthodox and unorthodox churches and cults, in feeling, tone, and vestiges of homeopathic and sympathetic magic, or in the shout songs of Black churches, no anthropologist really knows. Now it is generally known, however, that these cults were established in South America in Brazil and Venezuela, and particularly in the Caribbean island of Haiti. The American language has been greatly enriched with words of African origin, as the colorful words from the streets and the colonized ghettoes still keep the American language fluid and dynamic. Black America is tied to her ancient African heritage in all her physical and cultural manifestations.

Insofar as literature is created, evaluated, analyzed, and synthesized, Black writers have produced in the United States a literature that can be considered in terms of form and content, language, style, and tone, as can every other variety of world literature. If one is aware that Black writers are sometimes inclined, or directed by their white American education, toward an Anglo-Saxon tradition rather than their own Afro-American tradition, then analysis of subject matter and form should not be difficult. When we speak in the vernacular of our people, when we deal with folkways, folk beliefs, folk sayings; when we revolt against form and create new rhythms, improvise as the jazz musicians do, sing the blues, or dance the limbo, then we are dealing with an idiom that is most indigenous to Black people: always natural, freely experimental, always humanistic, most of all authentic of what is most real in the Black experience, then we are following an ancient tradition that is definitely not Anglo-Saxon.

As for poetic form, Black writers have experimented with all forms and with no traditional form. Afro-American literature in its most indigenous expression is not written in any Anglo-Saxon form, but takes the form of all oriental literature (this is particularly true of the poetry), that literature from which all western writers have copied or modified forms, the free alliterative verse that includes the use of any or all devices used to get music into free verse along with the key to wisdom literature—that key of parallelism of structure and thought.

The folk ballad is not as Oriental as that free line of alliterative verse, but it is still the oldest form of poetry. The Arabs were masters of the nomadic song, the love lyric, and the song of praise (more than 3,000 years of songs of praise exist); all Asia and Africa sang before the Saxons recorded their epics and romances. The Black writer in the United States does have a heritage, a literary heritage as ancient as the first record of life; and in a new land, in a strange land, even as slaves, Black people sang songs in a new language and made a new art to express their pain.

As students of Afro-American literature read this body of material, particularly the poetry, they will understand what is meant by a natural gift of song; they will discover individual voices speaking in each separate piece one's tongue, one's own vernacular, and one's adopted language to which Black people contributed.

From the eighteenth century until the present the student of Afro-American literature can trace the problems of Black people and see suffering transmuted into song—not always a song of love or joy, not always a cry of pain; sometimes a stern impassioned plea for justice, sometimes a bitter note of anger, sometimes a questioning or begging the question of Black humanity; sometimes the rousing note of social protest against slums and poverty, substandard education and housing, disease, slavery, discrimination, and war. But throughout this literature there is a record of what life has been for Black people in America for 350 years. It is also a remarkable affirmation of the human spirit that does prevail against all odds. To me, it is not nearly so remarkable that God could make a poet Black, as Countee Cullen says, and bid him sing; for song is his gift, as Du Bois reminds us; what is most remarkable is that his song can rise above the tragic world in which he lives and can transcend his misery. As Dunbar says:

> I know why the caged bird sings, ah me,
>   When his wing is bruised and his bosom sore,—
> When he beats his bars and would be free,
> It is not a carol of joy or glee,
>   But a prayer that he sends from his heart's deep core,
> But a plea, that upward to Heaven he flings—
> I know why the caged bird sings![1]

In their literary contributions to American culture, the Black writers have remained singularly faithful to the living truth of the human spirit. In a constant search for freedom, peace, and human dignity the Black writer has continued to speak loudly against social injustice, human slavery, open oppression of mind and body, violent intimidation, and humiliating indignities. Afro-American literature, art, music, and religious expression are full of these universal aspirations for truth and freedom. Not only do they celebrate life; these are celebrations of humanity and the highest essence of human spirit.

Whether we begin with the slave narrative of antebellum days and the life and times of Frederick Douglass, or the poetry of Phillis Wheatley and Frances Harper, we can hear this stirring cry for freedom, justice, and simple dignity. These are the words of Douglass at the end of one of the most eloquent slave narratives ever written:

> Sincerely and earnestly hoping that this little book may do something toward throwing light on the American slave system, and hastening the glad day of deliverance to the millions of my brethren in bonds—faithfully relying upon the power of truth, love, and justice, for success in my humble efforts—and solemnly pledging myself anew to the sacred cause, I subscribe myself, FREDERICK DOUGLASS; Lynn, Mass., April 28, 1845.[2]

And remember, it was also Douglass who said, "He who would be free must strike the first blow himself."

Let us not forget the words of another Black literary spokesman, Martin Delany, medical doctor, novelist, and political figure of no small stature during Reconstruction. When the fugitive slave bill was passed, Delany spoke to the mayor of Pittsburgh in a public address:

> If any man approaches that house in search of a slave—I care not who he may be, whether constable or sheriff, magistrate or even a judge of the Supreme Court—nay, let it be he who sanctioned this act to become a law, surrounded by his cabinet as his bodyguard . . . if he crosses the threshold of my door, and I do not lay him a lifeless corpse at my feet, I hope the grave

may refuse my body a resting place, and righteous Heaven my spirit a home.[3]

And in a more poetic vein the poignant voice of Phillis Wheatley (circa 1773):

> Should you, my Lord while you pursue my song
> Wonder from whence my love of *Freedom* sprung,
> Whence flow these wishes for the common good,
> By feeling hearts alone best understood,
> I, young in life, by seeming cruel fate
> Was snatch'd from *Alfric's* fancy'd happy seat:
> What pangs excruciating must molest,
> What sorrows labour in my parent's breast?
> Steel'd was the soul and by no misery mov'd
> That from a father seiz'd his babe belov'd:
> Such, such my case. And can I then but pray
> Others may never feel tyrannic sway?[4]

Or the proud appeal of Frances Harper in "Bury Me in a Free Land" (1854):

> Make me a grave where'er you will,
> In a lowly plain, or a lofty hill
> Make it among earth's humblest graves,
> But not in a land where men are slaves.
>
> I could not rest if around my grave
> I heard the steps of a trembling slave:
> His shadow above my silent tomb
> Would make it a place of fearful gloom. . . .
>
> I ask no monument, proud and high,
> To arrest the gaze of the passers-by;
> All that my yearning spirit craves,
> Is bury me not in a land of slaves.[5]

In more recent years at least two famous Black American writers have cried in a loud voice for all the world to hear. First, Richard Wright in *White Man, Listen!* (in the 1950s):

> I say to you white men of the West: Don't be too proud of how easily you conquered and plundered those Asians and Africans. . . . You must realize that it was not your courage or racial superiority that made you win, nor was it the racial inferiority or cowardice of the Asians and Africans that made them lose. . . .

Your world of culture clashed with the culture worlds of colored mankind, and the ensuing destruction of traditional beliefs among a billion and a half of black, brown, and yellow men has set off a tide of social, cultural, political, and economic revolution that grips the world today. That revolution is assuming many forms, absolutistic, communistic, fascistic, theocratistic etc.—all marked by unrest, violence, and an astounding emotional thrashing about as men seek new objects about which they can center their loyalties.[6]

Second, James Baldwin in *The Fire Next Time*:

If we—and now I mean the relatively conscious whites and the relatively conscious Blacks, who must, like lovers, insist on, or create, the consciousness of the others—if we do not falter in our duty now, we may be able, handful that we are, to end the racial nightmare, and achieve our country, and change the history of the world. If we do not now dare everything, the fulfillment of that prophecy, recreated from the Bible in song by a slave, is upon us: God gave Noah the rainbow sign, no more water, the fire next time![7]

J. A. Williams more recently has written, both in *The Man Who Cried I Am* and in *This Is My Country, Too*, similar sentiments. John O. Killens follows the same idea in *Black Man's Burden*.[8]

When I was a young woman, about twenty years of age, I went to speak to a group of white Methodists one Sunday afternoon in Illinois. They were interested in hearing about my growing up as a Methodist in the South before going off to school at Northwestern University. Afterward a woman came up to ask me a question. She wanted to know if I was bitter because I am a Negro. Her question shocked me profoundly, and I could only stammer out a hasty "No!" Later I brooded over her reasons or motives for such a question, but I was much older before I fully realized her complete lack of understanding and sense of common humanity. For her, racism was a deeply ingrained fact; race, to her, was the difference between pride and shame, between beauty and ugliness. Race was the whole meaning of her life, and humanity was beyond her comprehension because she had grown up in a society where race supersedes humanity. She felt sorry for me and believed that I was spiritually and physically scarred because I am Black. She was so completely foreign to the nature of my feelings that for a long time I could not fully comprehend her meaning or why she asked me such an awful, or stupid, question. My pity for her comes late in my life, now that I realize she was typical of much of white America and its failure to understand other human beings because of a segregationist philosophy and racist society.

The Black writer has repeatedly tried to speak to this problem; moreover, to speak to the human condition whether it is one of slave or free person, bondage of the mind, or spirit rather than of the body, or the question of peace, justice, and freedom, or evil in the world and suffering as a part of human existence. In the hundreds of novels written by Black authors over more than a century, several themes are outstanding, but the theme of miscegenation and race stands out first. It colored most of the early novels. Next came the theme of social protest; then the themes of the violent society versus the beleaguered individual; and finally, the theme of the adventurous emigrant who migrates in search of economic opportunity, political freedom, justice in the courts, and a better education for the children only to find, whether north, west, or east, the old protagonist of the human spirit against the dehumanizing factors of industry, machines, and money.

No one questions the deep pathos of our sorrow songs sung in a minor key, the feeling-tone of our religious and gospel music, the melancholy note in our blues, or the rhythmic syncopation of our jazz; but what most white America still does not know is that our literature reveals how we have transmuted suffering into song and heartbreak into compassion. Zora Neale Hurston combined a rich knowledge of folklore and humor in her tales of love and superstition, and Langston Hughes was the humanist par excellence—loving all mankind and celebrating life with a constant plea for social justice and a tender note of compassion for all the suffering poor. The Black writer therefore has a heritage of fighting for freedom, for the liberation of mind and spirit from the hideous bondage of racism and all the shackles of fearful prejudice. We have a rich gift for America, but it is a spiritual gift; and the materialists can neither understand and accept, nor benefit from such a gift. It is a gift of wholeness from within, born out of our ancient heritage and from the unbroken tradition of humanistic values that did not spring from Renaissance Europe, but developed in Asia and Africa before the religious wars of the Middle Ages. This humanism includes a recognition that we are part of nature and the historical process, that we are implicit in the dynamic evolving of mankind to ever higher planes of being, that all life must be richly developed in spirit rather than mere matter, and that one must regard the sacred nature of a brother or sister as one values his own privacy and inner sanctity. This religiosity has nothing to do with puritanism or with protestant obsession with sin. That is pure Anglo-Saxon religious trapping and not African at all. Snatched from an earthy animistic religious culture, our moral values are a far cry from the "pride" of the western world.

If we seemed to lose our cultural values in slavery and segregation, our youth today refuse to accept that loss, and they seek such values again.

Afro-Americans know why the quality of life in America has gone sour. It is because U.S. values are based on money and industry. It is because racism, militarism, materialism, and financial imperialism have gained a stronghold on this society like an octopus, and they are squeezing the life out of this nation before our very eyes. But we Black people are truly your metaphor. Richard Wright has said that the Negro is America's metaphor and I will say it as a simile. As fortune goes with us so goes the fortune of this nation. We are not playing a numbers game with destiny. The so-called silent majority will not survive catastrophe at the expense of the minority. Many are all upset now about the business of the environment, about ecology, about pollution . . . all types of pollution except mental pollution. We do not expect to walk quietly into crematories or into concentration camps. Do not say it cannot happen . . . because it did! But the whole world was not watching Germany on television. The Black minority, tragic though its lot may be, is not willing to succumb quietly to genocide. Claude McKay tells it as it is in his poem "If We Must Die":

If we must die, let it not be like hogs
Hunted and penned in an inglorious spot,
While round us bark the mad and hungry dogs
Making their mock at our accursed lot.
If we must die—O let us nobly die,
So that our precious blood may not be shed
In vain; then even the monsters we defy
Shall be constrained to honor us though dead!
O kinsmen! we must meet the common foe;
Though far outnumbered let us show us brave,
And for their thousand blows deal one deathblow!
What though before us lies the open grave?
Like men we'll face the murderous, cowardly pack,
Pressed to the wall, dying, but fighting back![9]

Yes, change is inevitable. Melvin Tolson has written a poem entitled "Dark Symphony," and in the grand finale of the last movement he says:

Out of abysses of Illiteracy,
Through labyrinths of Lies,
Across waste lands of Disease . . .
We advance!

Out of dead-ends of Poverty,
Through wildernesses of Superstition,
Across barricades of Jim Crowism . . .
We advance!

With the Peoples of the World . . .
We advance![10]

I would not be true to the humanistic tradition of Afro-American literature were I pessimistic about the goodness of the future. Change will come and there is hope for a better world. But that world must be founded on a new humanism instead of the old racism. In the twenty-first century perhaps the problem will no longer be that of the color line. There must be a new humanism. A new respect for the quality of all human life must be bred in our young. A new respect for humanity will outlaw war and hate and create new values that do not depend upon money and industry. Some of us are too old and too set in our minds to understand how far-reaching a change of social, mental, and spiritual climate is needed in this country. For some of us this means a whole new world brought on by violent confrontation and social upheaval, and since we are too old, we are afraid of that. But our children are not too young. They deserve a new mind to face a new universe.

Cultural change like social change depends upon reeducation. Religion, language, communications media, art, music, and literature are cultural instruments that must reeducate all our children with new values for a new century of a new humanism. Racism and racist theories of superiority and inferiority belong to the jungle of ignorant barbarism. They take us back to a time when men swung from trees like monkeys. This racism is a cancerous sore in American life that touches every phase of our living, and must be destroyed. All of us want to come out of the caves and stand erect and tall in the blinding light of day. Reeducation is the answer. Before we destroy our planet earth, in the words of the prophet Isaiah, come now and let us reason together. Mind and gray matter are the basics we need to use. Every child inherits a brain, a physical brain. Every human being has a spiritual entity. These are our inherent gifts with which to face the world, to deal with nature, and cooperate in a self-creating, reproducing society of humans. Humanity is our nature. Humanism is our natural philosophy. Since we are part of history, we are the historical process. When we know these truths, we are moving toward that noumenal world of freedom. Freedom comes from truth and the knowledge of truth is divine.

A *Message All Blackpeople Can Dig*
(& a few negroes too)
we are going to do it.
Us: Blackpeople, beautiful people; the sons and daughters
    of beautiful people.
bring it back to
US: the unimpossibility.
now is
the time, the test
while there is something to save (other than our lives).

we'll move together
hands on weapons & families
blending into the sun,
into each/other.
we'll love,
we've always loved.
just be cool & help one/another.
go ahead.
walk a righteous direction
under the moon,
in the night
bring new meanings to
the north star,
the Blackness,
to US.

discover new stars:
Street-light stars that will explode into evil-eyes,
light-bulb stars visible only to the realpeople,
clean stars, african & asian stars,
black aesthetic stars that will damage the whitemind;
killer stars that will move against
the unpeople.

came
brothers/fathers/sisters/mothers/sons/daughters
dance as one
walk slow & hip.
hip to what life is
and can be.
& remember we are not hippies,

WE WERE BORN HIP.
walk on, smile a little
yeah, that's it beautiful people
move on in, take over. take over, take over take/over
       takeovertakeovertakeover
     takeovertakeover, overtakeovertakeovertake over/
      take over take, over take,
        over take, over take.
Blackpeople
are moving, moving to return
    this earth into the hands of
human beings.[11]

Freedom, peace, and human dignity are only possible in a world where common humanity supersedes race. Spiritual entities cannot be attained by materialistic measures. Humans must learn to appreciate the spiritual nature and destiny of all people. There are all kinds of dogs and cats and horses in the world. But dogs do not get angry because all dogs are not Airedales or German shepherds or Pekingese. Why should people be more stupid than dogs, cats, or horses? It is time to leave pure animal matter and begin to rise above the flesh into the light of mind and spirit. How can one develop this new consciousness? It must be inbred and taught to our young. Children and youth today are adults tomorrow. The role of the school is superseded only by the home, and books are of infinite importance. What children read and see feed their minds in the same manner as what they eat feed their bodies. Afro-American literature is a reservoir of Black humanism. All America needs to become acquainted with this literature. White America still does not seem to understand that no people can enslave others' bodies and save their own souls. When every human being is holy in the eyes of another, then begins the millennium. Meanwhile, prepare for Armageddon.

Notes

1. Paul Laurence Dunbar, "Sympathy" from *Lyrics of the Heartside*, in *The Complete Poems of Paul Laurence Dunbar* (New York: Dodd, Mead and Company, 1913), p. 102.

2. Frederick Douglass, *Narrative of the Life of Frederick Douglass, an American Slave, Written by Himself* (Boston: Anti-Slavery Office, 1845; reprint ed., Garden City, New York: Anchor Press/Doubleday, 1973), p. 124.

3. Martin Delany quoted in *The Negro Caravan*, eds. Sterling Brown, Arthur P. Davis, and Ulysses Lee (1941; reprint ed., New York: Arno Press, 1969), p. 151.

4. Phillis Wheatley, "To the Right Honourable William, Earl of Dartmouth, His

Majesty's Principal Secretary of State for North America, &c." from *Poems on Various Subjects, Religious and Moral* (as originally appeared in 1773 edition published by A. Bell, London) in *The Collected Works of Phillis Wheatley*, ed. John C. Shields, The Schomburg Library of Nineteenth-Century Black Women Writers (New York: Oxford University Press, 1988), p. 74.

5. Frances E. W. Harper, "Bury Me in a Free Land" from *The Complete Poems of Frances E. W. Harper*, ed. Maryemma Graham, The Schomburg Library of Nineteenth-Century Black Women Writers (New York: Oxford University Press), pp. 93–4.

6. Richard Wright, *White Man, Listen* (New York: Doubleday, 1964; reprint ed., Westport, Conn.: Greenwood Press, 1978), pp. 22–30.

7. James Baldwin, *The Fire Next Time* (1963; reprint ed., New York: Dell 1970), p. 141.

8. John A. Williams, *The Man Who Cried I Am* (Boston: Little, Brown, 1967), and *This Is My Country, Too* (New York: New American Library, 1966), and John O. Killens, *Black Man's Burden* (New York: Simon and Schuster, 1965).

9. Claude McKay, *Selected Poems of Claude McKay* (New York: Harcourt, Brace & World, Inc., 1953), p. 36.

10. Melvin Tolson, *Rendevous with America*, (New York: Dodd, Mead and Company, 1944), pp. 41–2.

11. Don L. Lee, *Don't Cry, Scream* (Detroit: Broadside Press, 1970), pp. 63–4.

A Brief Introduction to Southern Literature

Some of the most distinguished names in literature, in America and in the world at large, are names of southerners of the U.S.A. Because of the nature of more than three hundred years of southern history, the student of American literature tends not to think of the hundreds of writers, Black and white, who were born in the South and claim this region for their native homes, regardless of whether, for one reason or another, they have gone outside the region to develop their writing aptitudes and practice the craft and art of writing.

If we could dispense altogether with regionalism in American literature and see America as a whole, we would have achieved the impossible, for each region has had its place in the sun insofar as American literature is concerned. Scholars speak of the American Renaissance when they mean a resurgence and awakening in New England with the transcendentalists; Hamlin Garland is a name to conjure with in the Midwest, as are Carl Sandburg and Sherwood Anderson. The West claims John Steinbeck and Walter van Tilburg Clark, author of *The Ox-Bow Incident*. I wish I could do justice to the hundreds of names in southern fiction, from John Pendleton Kennedy's *Swallow Barn* (1832) to Margaret Mitchell's *Gone with the Wind*

A version of this essay was presented at the Mississippi Arts Festival in Jackson, Mississippi, in 1971.

(1936) or from John William DeForest's *Miss Ravenel's Conversion* (1867) to my own *Jubilee* (1966), but that is an impossible task. The history and the literature of the South are a reflection of the life of the people, and the people have had too varied and too myriad an experience for me to deal with boldly and comprehensively. Therefore, I can at best attempt only a brief introduction to this literature.

As early as Kennedy's *Swallow Barn*, a southern tradition existed in American literature. That tradition became known as the plantation tradition, from which came both Paul Laurence Dunbar and Margaret Mitchell, with many others in between. The realm of Black and white minstrels belongs to this tradition. Dialect in its various manifestations was the language most familiar and typical. This marked the beginning of a set of stereotypes from which the literature has yet to free itself. Along with this plantation tradition, both Black and white writers have developed a folk tradition that began in the oral tradition of spirituals, work songs, and ballads. All this was essentially southern. America as a whole became enthralled with southern manners, language, and scenery when Mark Twain, with his Mississippi River stories, opened a classic new chapter in American literature, immortalizing that section of the country from St. Louis to New Orleans. The riverboat, life on the Mississippi, the water commerce, these have contributed to the color not only of the region but of all American literature. New Orleans, Memphis, Charleston, and Atlanta have been at one time or another the queen cities of southern literature, but the rural South is equally as popular.

It is impossible to read our most distinguished writers without being conscious at once of the land as well as the people. The love of the southerner for the land—the southern soil—and the strange agrarian beliefs of such groups of southern writers as the Vanderbilt group, all these have given rise to stories with settings ranging from Texas to the Carolinas and the Gulf Coast through the mountains of Tennessee and Kentucky. There is not a southern state that has not figured prominently in literature. Perhaps in its most striking sense the South has agonized through the Civil War battlegrounds and scenes more than any other region, for this war has seemed most particularly the southern war—the "only war"—and is often considered the southern *Iliad*.

But, what the world knows of this literature, it knows in two widely differing segments. Some of southern literature is known, even at home, scarcely at all because of the nature of the institutions of slavery and segregation. Comparisons between Black writers and white writers can be made in terms of period, subject matter, and form. When this is done, one begins to see more than one side, or facet, of an interesting American theme. During the summer of 1963, a violent year of the sixties in America, I had the rare privilege of taking a course in southern literature under Professor Arlin Turner of Duke University who was teaching that summer in Iowa, and I found myself rereading the fiction of my adolescence, and discovering I had cut my teeth on much of southern fiction, both Black and white. Black writers like Langston Hughes and Arna Bontemps and Zora Neale Hurston were born in the South; white writers like Thomas Wolfe and DuBose Heyward and Julia Peterkin, Caroline Gordon, Ellen Glasgow and Mary Rinehart Roberts had provided me with many a summer's reading. Books like *Black Is My True-Love's Hair* (Elizabeth Maddox Roberts), *Lamb in His Bosom* (Carolin Pafford Miller), *None Shall Look Back* (Caroline Gordon), and *So Red the Rose* (Stark Young), were just as familiar as Hughes's *Not without Laughter*, Bontemps's *Black Thunder*, and Hurston's *Jonah's Gourd Vine.*[1] The southern writer, like all American writers, but perhaps with more intensity, deals largely with race. He or she cannot escape the ever present factor of race and the problems of race as they have grown out of the southern society and affected all of America. The treatment first of the Black man, or the Negro, in southern fiction has been not only the problem of character delineation but also the moral problem of race. The subject of race has been romanticized, and realistically portrayed, and the characters have ranged from wooden stereotypes—flat, mindless, and caricatured as buffoons—to deft and skillful portrayal of both realistic and humanistic proportions. The subject of race has become theme and conflict and character development in southern literature.

Perhaps the single most glaring fault Black Americans find with southern literature by white writers is in the psychology and philosophy, which of necessity in most instances is racist. This has to be understood in terms of the society, the values emphasized in American education, the nature of slavery and segregation, which not only have kept the races apart, separated and polarized in two segregated societies but have ostracized the artistic accomplishments of Black people and ignored their literature. The earliest writers, Black and white, were fighting a racial battle, the white writers were writing apologies for slavery and the Black writers were protesting against the inhumanity of the slave system. With the substitution of segregation, the white child was educated to regard race as more important than humanity and the Black child was educated to imitate a white world as superior to his and thus taught to hate himself. The battle and the conflict can be seen in the literature.

John Esten Cooke, William Gilmore Simms, and Thomas Nelson Page obviously present an altogether different picture from Frederick Douglass, Martin DeLany, and Frances Watkins Harper. Cooke, Simms, and Page served as agents for antebellum southern planter ideals. Their dialect stories, written in the local color tradition, were uncritical in their acceptance of the southern aristocracy that maintained an oppressive slave system. Douglass, DeLany, and Harper, on the other hand, strongly advocated abolishing slavery and found nothing in the slave system to sentimentalize.

Mark Twain's Huck Finn and Jim provide another profile of the treatment of race in southern and American literature. While Twain moved away from the conventions of the sentimental novel, his adaptations of southern humor created Jim and Huck Finn as outsider figures, thus giving way to a new stereotype.

James Russell, Joel Chandler Harris, and Augustus Baldwin Longstreet should be compared with Paul Laurence Dunbar, James Weldon Johnson, and Charles Chestnutt. Harris, Russell, and Longstreet strived to be true to the manners, language and attitudes of their characters. For them, Black nature was not something to be scoffed at or derided, but was a distinctive, if not peculiar, feature of the South. They were among the earliest white writers to recognize the immense creative possibilities of the Black folk expression that Dunbar, Chestnutt, and Johnson used in their works. George Washington Cable and Albion Tourgee are fit writers to compare with W. E. B. Du Bois and the Joseph Seaman Cotters, junior and senior. Cable and Tourgee were the most politically conscious among postbellum white writers. One notes a tinge of social reformism in their work that echoes the concerns of Du Bois and other Black political leaders.

Reading Mark Twain's stories as a child I came across the word *nigger* and put the book down. Years later hearing the ironic incident told as a joke I could not laugh: "Heard about a terrible accident," and one asked, "Did anybody get hurt?" "Nome, just killed a nigger." The full implication was that a Black man was not a human being and this was the racist problem of early southern literature. But it is also important to relate here by the same token much of American literature outside the South did not move me at all. If the South seemed obsessed by race, at least it was a subject. Hemingway's fiction was certainly not as immediate and meaningful, for that same reason, as Faulkner's was to me.

When one thinks of southern literature, the sentimental tradition of moonlight and roses, magnolias and mockingbirds, comes to mind as a definite part of our southern heritage in American literature. But the violent South is a theme that is also evident in southern and American literature from the days of the frontier through the Civil War to the days of the Civil Rights Movement. The violent South gives rise to certain aspects as part of the history of American literature: the Gothic novel, which includes the grotesque, the macabre, the supernatural (such as ghosts); the violence so characteristic in southern fiction is easily accommodated within the Gothic tradition. Edgar Allan Poe is perhaps the single most important figure who influenced a whole school of poetry, the Symbolists, in France including Mallarmé, Rimbaud, Valéry, and Baudelaire. With the southern writer, we automatically think of Poe's tales of ratiocination and mystery when we also think of the Gothic novels of Carson McCullers, Flannery O'Conner, and Alice Walker and the prose of today.

When one reads McCullers, the world becomes inhabited by the isolated; by the lonely vainly groping for escape, as shown in *The Heart Is a Lonely Hunter* (1940). Her world is also one of thwarted homosexuality (*Reflections in a Golden Eye*, 1941); of the physically and emotionally misshapen (*The Ballad of the Sad Cafe*, 1951); or of the ache of the dailiness of life (the autobiographical *The Member of the Wedding*, 1946). All are bound by the chord of disjunction, of virulent loneliness. Little sunshine penetrates her dark and Gothic universe. Hope appears to have fled.

With the writers Flannery O'Connor and Alice Walker the landscape is not as sere. But although O'Connor and Walker "lived within minutes of each other on the same Eatonton to Milledgeville road,"[2] they differ in race, in religion, and in thematic treatment. There are, however, areas of likeness. Both offer a somewhat more hopeful picture of life, and both appear to infuse their characters with elements of realism. Black writer Walker has observed that when O'Connor wrote "not a whiff of magnolia hovered in the air."[3] Walker found in O'Connor a truth that surpasses race, thereby achieving a widened vision of the universe: "But essential O'Connor is not about race at all . . . it is 'about' the impact of supernatural grace on human beings."[4]

While O'Connor's characters are mutilated by their quests for salvation (i.e., a seeking for divine mercy from an unyielding God) as shown in the character Motes in *Wise Blood* (1952) and Tarwater in *The Violent Bear It Away* (1960), Walker's protagonists are oppressed from within and from without. Theirs is a universe tyrannized by the rejection of white society (without), and more crucially, Black self-dehumanization (within). *The Third Life of Grange Copeland* (1970) illustrates this two-pronged oppression through three generations. At the core of the oppression is the Black woman—rejected by white society, while being abused by Black men. Such a bitter vision thwarts and twists hopes and dreams. In her award-winning *The Color Purple*, Walker's protagonist, Celie, frees herself from oppression based on race, on sex, and on physical appearance. Unlike O'Connor's God, Walker's God, in *The Color Purple*, can rejoice with woman,[5] thereby freeing her to love and to seek that which liberates and fulfills. Walker thus breaks from O'Connor and McCullers by rejecting the Gothic view and permitting the terror and evil in the world to be overcome by her characters.

It is in William Faulkner, Eudora Welty, and Richard Wright that we see the southern writer rising above time and place, struggling beyond the racist limitations of his or her society into the truly rarified world of the artist, a world in which human values and universal truths take precedence over provincial and philistine notions and bigoted minds. In his acceptance speech for the Nobel prize, William Faulkner expressed his belief in the need of the writer to lift up the human heart in order for the human spirit to struggle to prevail, to triumph over all. Like all great writers they move from the local to the universal, from the immediate to the timeless, and from the simple into the sublime. William Faulkner, Richard Wright, and Eudora Welty are among the most modern of American writers whose native home is the South, and particularly Mississippi. They differ widely in their writings, but they have certain verities in common. They deal with the southern scene; they deal with a violent South, too, but they also work within the framework of a humanistic tradition.

William Faulkner's writing shows a multiracial and multiclass consciousness. Faulkner considers three races in his native Mississippi. His approach is the traditional, such as in all the hackneyed themes of miscegenation and the tragic mulatto, and yet he is innovative and experimental as well. He deals with the southern landscape in a meaningful fashion, and as a symbolist he creates a fictitious world that thoroughly absorbs the American myth about race. Yoknapatawpha is more than the creation of Faulkner's imagination, it is a re-creation of a real southern county in which he lived, as well as a microcosm of much of America on the subject of race.

Eudora Welty skillfully expresses the folk life of her place and time, but she moves beyond these into eternal and universal truths of the human spirit. Like many other people, my favorite short stories are "Why I Live at the P.O." and "A Worn Path." Here she expresses the fundamental philosophies of simple people in an unerring and unforgettable fashion, using humor and pathos without undue sentimentality. I am sure she would not like to be labeled as a member of the Faulkner school when she is also so unlike him, and would doubtless prefer to be associated with the name of Katherine Ann Porter, who has won recognition throughout the world for her craftsmanship as a short story writer. She may have been Miss Welty's teacher, but then often the pupil equals if not surpasses the teacher. Welty's recent novels suggest that indeed she has. I am also sure if you asked Miss Welty about her treatment of race she would say she does no such thing, she writes about people. And therein lies the secret of greatness. The writer is concerned with the human condition. He or she writes about people as people, not as things. Welty sees race superseded by humanity, and as such, she values the human spirit above everything else.

Richard Wright spent his last years far from Mississippi but all that he wrote of significance and strength, and he was a powerful writer, make no mistake about that—power and passion he had—all that he wrote grows out of those nineteen years of his life he spent in the South. The violent South left an indelible impression upon him, and all the rest of his life he was struggling to express the need for men to understand the highest human values as superior to the bigoted notions of race, class, creed and any other prejudices that hinder the human spirit and cloud the human intelligence.

The South has produced a great body of literature, despite all the social hindrances of what James W. Silver calls a "closed society."[6] The South is not alone guilty in terms of racism. All America today suffers from the sickness of racism. All America today also suffers from paranoia. White America seems to have the strange sickness of delusions of grandeur while Black Americans seem to suffer from delusions of persecution. None of us is willing to believe any of it is only a delusion. But our literature reflects our society, and when we are a polarized or segregated society, our literature is also. We would hope for a healing of our sick society, sick of war and division, sick of material values and a quality of life gone sour with pollution, with militarism, racism, and materialism. Our hope for the future must be with the proverbial madmen of the world—the priests and the poets, and the lovers. All of them are mad, drunk with love and religion and the smoke of inspiration. But the artists have always been, too, the avant garde. They have the ideas that the philosophers generate, and they implement the new concepts of the universe in order that man may build a better society. It is therefore in the literature of today that we have cultural hope for change tomorrow. Literature is a cultural instrument, and as such, we build toward a new twenty-first century that will have learned all the sad lessons of the twentieth century. Perhaps we will produce together all that is needed for one race on the face of the earth, the human race.

Two poems express for me the strong sense of the South as I have known and experienced it. I wrote them when I was quite young and a long way from home. "Southern Song" and "Sorrow Home" are from my first book of poems, *For My People*:

Southern Song

I want my body bathed again by southern suns, my soul
    reclaimed again from southern land. I want to rest
    again in southern fields, in grass and hay and clover
    bloom; to lay my hand again upon the clay baked by
    a southern sun, to touch the rain-soaked earth and
    smell the smell of soil.

I want my rest unbroken in the fields of southern earth;
    freedom to watch the corn wave silver in the sun and
    mark the splashing of a brook, a pond with ducks
    and frogs and count the clouds.

I want no mobs to wrench me from my southern rest; no
    forms to take me in the night and burn my shack and
    make for me a nightmare full of oil and flame.

I want my careless song to strike no minor key; no fiend to
    stand between my body's southern song—the fusion of the
    South, my body's song and me.

Sorrow Home

My roots are deep in southern life; deeper than John Brown
    or Nat Turner or Robert Lee. I was sired and weaned
    in a tropic world. The palm tree and banana leaf,
    mango and coconut, breadfruit and rubber trees
    know me.

Warm skies and gulf blue streams are in my blood. I belong
    with the smell of fresh pine, with the trail of coon,
    and the spring growth of wild onion.

I am no hot-house bulb to be reared in steam-heated flats
    with the music of "L" and subway in my ears, walled
    in by steel and wood and brick far from the sky.

I want the cotton fields, tobacco and the cane. I want to walk
    along with sacks of seed to drop in fallow ground.

Restless music is in my heart and I am eager to be
gone. O Southland, sorrow home, melody beating in my bone and
blood! How long will the Klan of hate, the hounds
and the chain gangs keep me from my own?[7]

Notes

1. All of these books were published during the 1930s. I wish to acknowledge the white southern chronology from Turner's *Southern Stories* (New York: Holt, Rinehart, 1960), and the companion piece on events in the Negro world from *The Negro Caravan*, edited by Sterling Brown, Ulysses Lee, and Arthur P. Davis (New York: Arno Press, 1969).

2. Alice Walker, *In Search of Our Mother's Garden* (New York: Harcourt, Brace, 1983), p. 42.

3. Ibid., p. 52.

4. Ibid., p. 53.

5. Alice Walker, *The Color Purple* (New York: Washington Square Press, 1982), pp. 178, 179, 249.

6. *Mississippi: The Closed Society* (1964) (New enl. ed., New York: Harcourt, Brace & World, 1966) is a remarkable and revealing account of the desegregation of the South, written when Silver was then professor of history at the University of Mississippi.

7. *For My People* (New Haven: Yale University Press, 1942).

Faulkner and Race

William Faulkner's greatness may well be his unique achievement in incorporating the American myth about race and the Christian myth of redemption in a body of fiction that is symbolic, humanistic, timeless, and universal. He successfully communicates to his readers a sense of history combined with a deep-seated sense of morality or honor. His vision is tragicomic and his tradition is truly that of American Gothic. His use of symbol, myth, and legend is indisputably great. He is the only white American whose use of race and religion in literature can be said to plumb the depths of myth, which, of course, is the seedbed of both religion and literature.

Race in Faulkner's fiction is not limited to one racial group. He deals with three races in his native state—the red man, who was here first, the white man, whose threefold guilt obsesses him, and the Black man, who is a pawn, a type, a shapeless symbol, a victim or scapegoat, and who only occasionally achieves humanity. One must read a large body of Faulkner's fiction from the beginning to the end in order to understand even slightly his strange code of honor, his attitude about race, and his deeply religious commitment. Yet this morality, or moral concern about race, is stamped on every major work and

Reprinted and edited from *The Maker and the Myth*, pp. 105–21, edited by Evans Harrington and Ann J. Abadie (University Press of Mississippi, 1978), by permission of the publisher.

143

is especially thematic in the big body of his fiction. Some smaller pieces are even more perfected forms of this interest. "That Evening Sun" is notable, but the entire early collection *Go Down, Moses and Other Stories* deals with Faulkner's Negroes. Dilsey in *The Sound and the Fury*, Lucas Beauchamp in *Intruder in the Dust*, and Joe Christmas in *Light in August* are important racial characters. In "The Old People," "Red Leaves," and "The Bear," Faulkner emphasizes the Indians, but here there are also Black and white people.

The racial theme may best be understood in terms of the original Cain–Abel conflict, "Am I my brother's keeper?" Faulkner's symbol for universal man in southern society, and in time, all society, his condition is the man of mixed blood. In his early work these characters—and there are a number of them—are at war with self. The mulatto is a symbol for the problem of race relations—brother's abuse of brother—man against man.

In *Absalom, Absalom!* (1936), Charles Bon is a man of mixed blood who has chosen to identify with his white heritage. A white-Negro, he is a symbol of the spirit of the frontier and of the property consciousness of the white man. But, in spite of his choice, Bon is a symbol of the frustration of the mulatto because his father, the white planter, refuses to call Bon his son.

On the other hand, in *Go Down, Moses* (1942), Sam Fathers—whom the plantation owner McCaslin Edmonds thinks of as a tragic mulatto, a man at war within himself—is not tragic at all. He is really a man at peace with himself. In him (he is half Indian and half Negro) the blood has run Black. He is humble before nature—he is the only fit tutor for Ike, the potential heir of the plantation. It is Sam Fathers who teaches Ike what he needs to know to free himself from the curse of Israel, that of slavery—"Sam Fathers set me free," Ike tells McCaslin Edmonds ("The Bear").

The experience of discovering the source of the curse of slavery in the plantation legacy stimulates Ike to renounce his heritage. His discovery is a step-by-step process that allows him to progress backward beyond what "was," beyond his father's and uncle's world, and identify the first sin. He sees his grandfather Carothers McCaslin as a man with sin. It is not the miscegenation between Carothers and a slave that is wrong, but the incest between Carothers and the daughter produced by that act. Carothers uses his own daughter as a thing for his pleasure rather than as a daughter or even as human being, and thus violates her humanity in the most crass way Faulkner can imagine.

Other members of his family, Buck and Buddy, feel the guilt, but they perpetuate the legacy of man's crime against his fellowman for they are unable to totally liberate their slaves. Ike, here, finally recognizes that this is not just his grandfather's sin: "until at last he saw that they were all Grandfather all of them and that from even the best" ("Was," in Go Down, Moses).

Black students and even some whites who read "The Bear" may be bothered by some things in it that they see as racist. Faulkner was, in fact, a racist—but two or three things are important to note. First of all, he knew that and knew it thirty-five or forty years before anyone much talked in such terms. Second, he knew that the whole of American society in these United States—North and South—was racist. Third, he moved beyond where many people are today to discover that, in an important way, to say one is a racist is to say one is human and the product of his culture. Fourth, and most important, he did not conclude that this realization (that is to be racist is to be human) removed any of the guilt and responsibility from the perceiver. For Faulkner devoted a good share of his work, his ability, to the problem of coming to terms with his racism (in a social context). Learning this, and attempting to do something about it, is what "The Bear" is all about, particularly part five.

Faulkner's philosophy has often seemed puzzling, and in the early years of his career, must have been completely misunderstood, certainly by those few critics who first judged him as a Communist, a Socialist realist, or a naturalist such as Granville Hicks and, even later, by the New Critics from the Ivy League who began to read everything in terms of the Christian myth of redemption, pointing out epiphany, baptism, transfiguration, crucifixion, and resurrection in every Faulkner product. Faulkner has been treated as stoic humanist, Christian, and segregationist—the three are not necessarily compatible. For our purposes here, Faulkner is a symbolist treating characters as symbols and types, preferring to deal with the standards of life as human rather than divine or bestial, hating always the nonhuman, the mechanical, or mechanistic, and believing always in the human spirit, the human being, the human heart. Faulkner should be read as one reads the Bible—not literally but figuratively.

Whether his characters are red, Black, or white, they symbolize certain basic ideas, social classes, racial types, codes of honor, and traditional versus nontraditional standards or values. They are therefore symbols. Individuation and characters in the round may rarely be found in Faulkner. He is not concerned with delineating or developing character. Rather he reveals their shadowy shapes and even the names he gives them are symbolic: Nancy Mannigoe—who goes with many men; Lena Grove—the nature symbol, of a tree; Candace, or Candy—sweet and sexually seductive; The Snopses—

snooping and like swine, a pig's (snope) snout; Jesus—the Black cuckold husband of Nancy in "That Evening Sun"; Joe Christmas—the tragic mulatto and Christ figure.

Despite Faulkner's admission that demons drove him, we understand his complex genius as intuitive, insightful, and brooding, thoughtful genius together with the demonic and the orphic. We can thus begin to understand how the great welter of his imagination and his chief frame of reference must be his own family history, his familiar home surroundings, the people of his own town and county. What he called his postage stamp of the world in microcosm.

Just as Yoknapatawpha is not merely a creation or figment of his own imagination but in reality the country he has known all his life; his characters are, too, the same familiar people he has known in that country. That red men must be the same red men he has either known—or been accustomed to conceiving as such—as hunters, brave and courageous men, and men initiated into manhood through bravery and courage. The Black men are the menials or servant Negroes he has known, the suffering servants as in Isaiah, the prophet; the whites, rich and poor, are his own family and neighbors. Real and legendary, they do not come from another country.

If we first define the American myth about race and later explain the religious myth of Christian redemption as seen in Faulkner, we can perhaps understand the magnitude of his achievement.

Faulkner was born into a southern community in Mississippi, where racial attitudes, mores, and customs had crystallized into a pattern of social behavior for at least a hundred years. He was born into a racially segregated society, and all of his life he must have been a segregationist. The American myth about race is built around an idea of racial superiority and inferiority. The master race is superior to the slave race in such a philosophy. The slave race is not comprised of adult human beings but childlike, animal-like creatures who are seen possessing certain typical characteristics. In such a conceived body of thought the red man and Black man are primitives, untouched by the corrupting taint of civilization—savages but noble beings, nevertheless, born with natural honor and integrity. The civilized white man, however, is not a primitive; that is, he is not innocent. He has tasted the fruit of the tree of knowledge, of good and evil, and he is guilty of the sin of disobedience and is doomed to death. His guilt or sin is threefold in Faulknerian terms. He has sinned against nature or the land by abusing it; he has sinned against the red man by usurping his land and annihilating his people; and he has sinned against the Black man, not only by enslaving him, but also by violating Black women and thus bringing into existence the mixed breed, or mongrelized race of mixed blood. These are the sins, or crimes, between the white man and God. The white man has therefore lost honor and integrity and he is damned to the fires of hell. This should not be called merely a southern myth. It belongs to all white America and is as old as the nation itself.

Now, I must hasten to add that white Americans believing this myth are not aware that it is a myth nor how it became one. But how it became a myth is beside the point. This is the myth about race that Faulkner grew up hearing, believing, and having ingrained into him. His rational powers of thought may have questioned all the nuances of this racial rationalization, or rationale, for slavery and segregation, but as he says, "Memory believes before knowing remembers." Some critics offer an interesting theory of how Faulkner's fiction follows a line of growing awareness of humanity in the Black man.

Faulkner was not only born white in a segregated society comprised of three races—two regarded as inferior and one as superior—he was born in the Bible Belt where Christian honor, virtue, and integrity were standards accepted as ideal and perfect. Faulkner is therefore white segregationist and southern Christian. He is very much like the puritan Hawthorne in this respect. Faulkner's first book, *The Marble Faun*, a collection of poems, shows how Hawthorne influenced him. He is also deeply influenced by fundamentalism in religion, and the Protestant or Calvinist obsession with sin. Beginning with the Pentateuch, or Torah, the entrance of evil, or sin, and death into the world, the ideas of sacrifice from Abraham and Isaac to the New Testament of Jesus Christ as the Lamb of God—the whole story of sin and redemption may be seen transposed and sublimated into Faulkner's fiction. All-men-are-brothers-and-God-is-our-Father is an idea negated by racism or segregationist views of religion, of man, and God. A myth about race is absolutely necessary for such inherent contradictions in the society in order to mitigate them.

Faulkner's Negro characters are all tied to the myth of Christian redemption as surely as they are victims of the racial myth and segregated society. But Faulkner is quick to advance the theory that only in the racially mixed such as Joe Christmas in *Light in August* is there tragic conflict. Joe Christmas suffers because he lacks racial identity, and his tragedy is therefore the tragedy of miscegenation, or mixed blood.

But the honor of Faulkner's house of heroes or antiheroes is the honor of Christian integrity, an integrity violated by a breach of five of the Ten

Commandments: Thou shalt not steal; Thou shalt not kill; Thou shalt not commit adultery; Thou shalt not covet; Thou shalt not bear false witness, or Thou shalt not lie. But drunkenness, lying, incest, murder, rape, and swearing or cursing great oaths—all these are prevalent in the violent, Gothic, macabre atmosphere of Faulknerian fiction. Love, honor, integrity, reverence are not merely Old Testament commandments. These are Christian virtues.

The moral problem is therefore central in Faulkner. The moral problem of race is just as central as the religious problem of sin and redemption. The problem of evil is both the problem of sin and the shadow of race. And the two are constantly intertwined. Class is also very important to Faulkner. Quality white folks are not as dirty and low-down as low-class white folks. In Faulkner's Yoknapatawpha, old man Sutpen and the Snopeses are not in the same class with Colonel Sartoris, because they stooped to actions only inferior men would stoop to do, such as taking the so-called "wild" Negroes from Africa and beating them into submission and cheap labor as slaves in order to build plantations, estates, and material empires. Then as if this were not enough, compounded with the evil of slavery is the evil of miscegenation. Stooping to Black women is not only a racial sin but a sin against class and honor. Lynching and rape and miscegenation do not touch the garments of the rich until the whole white South is cursed by slavery. After the Civil War, decadence begins. Even the Compsons in *The Sound and the Fury* are cursed because of sexual greed and greed for money. These are the evil fruits of slavery. "Radix malorum est cupiditas," the root of evil is desire.

Dilsey from *The Sound and the Fury* and Joe Christmas in *Light in August* are frequently cited as Faulkner's greatest Black characters—but if you ask Black people, they would choose Lucas Beauchamp in *Intruder in the Dust*. Here for the first time in Faulkner's novels is a Black man with dignity, one who approaches if not achieves humanity. Dilsey is a type, and Christmas is a symbol, but Beauchamp is almost a man. Dilsey as a character is a flat, mindless stereotype. She is in the plantation tradition established by John Pendleton Kennedy's *Swallow Barn*. As a mammy, a faithful old retainer, she is unacceptable to the average Black reader as a real Black mother. It is one thing for her white folks to love her and for her to love their children—this is a carryover from the economic system of slavery—but it is utterly unnatural for her to mistreat her own child at the same time by calling him a fool. As a deeply religious person, fundamentalist in her faith, she would fear hellfire for calling anyone a fool. Because she is a domestic servant, because she is a menial, because she is a type, it is in the typical fashion of white American tradition to invest her with love, compassion, pity, and bravery. This is Faulkner's use of character in the traditional fashion. Perhaps he is influenced by his love for his own mammy, Caroline Barr. Perhaps the character of Dilsey is modeled after her and surely Faulkner felt deep affection for her as he must have felt she showed him love and kindness, genuine and sincerely felt; but insofar as greatness of being is concerned, Dilsey does not qualify as a great character merely because she was a servant. And she certainly was not humble. She not only ran her family and the Compsons—she knew she kept them together and she knew she was the boss, as demonstrated in this passage from *The Sound and the Fury*:

"Oh, Lawd," Dilsey said. She set the sifter down and swept up the hem of her apron and wiped her hands and caught up the bottle from the chair on which she had laid it and gathered her apron about the handle of the kettle which was now jetting faintly. "Jes a minute," she called. "De water jes dis minute got hot."

It was not the bottle which Mrs. Compson wanted however, and clutching it by the neck like a dead hen Dilsey went to the foot of the stairs and looked upward.

"Aint Luster up dar wid him?" she said.

"Luster hasn't been in the house. I've been lying here listening for him. I knew he would be late, but I did hope he'd come in time to keep Benjamin from disturbing Jason on Jason's one day in the week to sleep in the morning."

"I dont see how you expect anybody to sleep, wid you standin in de hall, holl'in at folks fum de crack of dawn," Dilsey said. She began to mount the stairs, toiling heavily. "I sont dat boy up dar half hour ago."

Mrs. Compson watched her, holding the dressing gown under her chin. "What are you going to do?" she said.

"Gwine git Benjy dressed en bring him down to de kitchen, whar he won't wake Jason en Quentin," Dilsey said.

"Haven't you started breakfast yet?"

"I'll tend to dat too," Dilsey said. "You better git back in bed twell Luster make yo fire. Hit cold dis mawnin."

"I know it," Mrs. Compson said. "My feet are like ice. They were so cold they waked me up." She watched Dilsey mount the stairs. It took her a long while. "You know how it frets Jason when breakfast is late," Mrs. Compson said.

"I cant do but one thing at a time," Dilsey said. "You git on back to bed, fo I has you on my hands dis mawnin too."

"If you're going to drop everything to dress Benjamin, I'd better come down and get breakfast. You know as well as I do how Jason acts when it's late."

"En who gwine eat yo messin?" Dilsey said. "Tell me dat. Go on now," she said, toiling upward. Mrs. Compson stood watching her as she mounted, steadying herself against the wall with one hand, holding her skirts up with the other.

There is no question that Faulkner progresses in his understanding of Black humanity as portrayed in his fictional characters who are Black. His Black trilogy really consists of *Light in August*, first published in 1932, followed by *Go Down, Moses* ten years later in 1942, and concludes with *Intruder in the Dust* in 1948. This last novel comes twenty-two years after his first novel, *Soldier's Pay*, and a little over a year before he won the Nobel Prize. There are two major characters concerned with race. One is Joe Christmas, who really does not know who he is and therein lies his tragedy— loss of identity, and alienation. The other is Lucas Beauchamp, who grows as a character in Faulkner's mind over some fourteen or fifteen years. He almost never begs the question of his humanity as Jesus's wife Nancy does (in the story "That Evening Sun," from the *Collected Stories*) when she says, "It's not my fault. I ain't nothing but a nigger." Lucas not only repeatedly asserts his manhood, but he also maintains it, acting with the dignity he feels befits his manhood. The tragic figure in "Pantaloon in Black" is exactly as Faulkner describes him, a clown, a buffoon, the typical minstrel type he is. He reminds us of the great Pagliacci. "Laugh, clown, laugh," even when your heart is breaking. The minstrel type, clown or buffoon, is exemplified in Rider of "Pantaloon in Black" in *Go Down, Moses*:

> "So Ketcham come on back down stairs and pretty soon the chain gang come in and went on up to the bull pen and he thought things had settled down for a while when all of a sudden he begun to hear the yelling, not howling: yelling, though there wasn't no words in it, and he grabbed his pistol and run back up stairs to the bull pen where the chain gang was and Ketcham could see into the cell where the old woman was kind of squinched down in one corner and where that nigger had done tore that iron cot clean out of the floor it was bolted to and was standing in the middle of the cell, holding the cot over his head like it was a baby's cradle, yelling, and says to the old woman, 'Ah aint goan hurt you,' and throws the cot against the wall and comes and grabs holt of that steel barred door and rips it out of the wall, bricks, hinges and all, and walks out of the cell toting the door over his head like it was a gauze window screen, hollering, 'It's awright. It's awright. Ah aint trying to git away.'
>
> "Of course Ketcham could have shot him right there, but like he said, if

it wasn't going to be the law, then them Birdsong boys ought to have the first lick at him. So Ketcham dont shoot. Instead, he jumps in behind where them chain gang niggers was kind of backed off from that steel door, hollering, 'Grab him! Throw him down!' except the niggers hung back at first too until Ketcham gets in where he can kick the ones he can reach, batting at the others with the flat of the pistol until they rush him. And Ketcham says that for a full minute that nigger would grab them as they come in and fling them clean across the room like they was rag dolls, saying, 'Ah aint tryin to git out. Ah aint tryin to git out,' until at last they pulled him down—a big mass of nigger heads and arms and legs boiling around on the floor and even then Ketcham says every now and then a nigger would come flying out and go sailing through the air across the room, spraddled out like a flying squirrel and with his eyes sticking out like car headlights, until at last they had him down and Ketcham went in and began peeling away niggers until he could see him laying there under the pile of them, laughing, with tears as big as glass marbles running across his face and down past his ears and making a kind of popping sound on the floor like somebody dropping bird eggs, laughing and laughing and saying, 'Hit look lack Ah just cant quit thinking. Look lack Ah just cant quit.' And what do you think of that?"

"I think if you eat any supper in this house you'll do it in the next five minutes," his wife said from the dining room. "I'm going to clear this table then and I'm going to the picture show."

So then, Faulkner runs the gamut from traditional to nontraditional treatment of Black characters. Blacks are equated first with animals—" 'Them damn niggers,' he said, 'I swear to godfrey, it's a wonder we have as little trouble with them as we do. Because why? Because they aint human. They look like a man and they walk on their hind legs like a man, and they can talk and you can understand them and you think they are understanding you, at least now and then. But when it comes to the normal human feelings and sentiments of human beings, they might just as well be a damn herd of wild buffaloes'" (*Go Down, Moses*)—considered wild savages, then children, then as stereotypes, then as clowns or buffoons, and only in Lucas Beauchamp does a Black man approach humanity. "I'm a nigger," Lucas said, "but I'm a man too" ("The Fire and the Hearth," in *Go Down, Moses*).

Faulkner tries to avoid the old stereotypes about race brought over from the plantation tradition, even though quite unconsciously he changes some of these old stereotypes into new stereotypes. He rejects the idea that all Negroes are lazy and nasty, thieves and rapists of white people. Faulkner's Negroes are more often victims of poor and lower-class Caucasians who are not above rape, murder, incest, and all such crimes of greed and passion. He maintains, however, most of the sexual stereotypes and taboos that have racial labels. He clings to the plantation ideas and stereotypes of the faithful old retainer, the Black wet nurse, the mammy, the kind of Negro represented by Dilsey. He invests her with dignity, love, compassion, and above all, the ability to endure and survive the outrage of slavery, servitude, and segregation. He either knows no educated Blacks or has no respect for them. He regards the Negro's adjustment and adaptability to western white world culture as superior to the inscrutable primitivism of the Indian, or red man, who insists on clinging to all the old ways of his dying culture and annihilated civilization. Faulkner does not accept any part of the red man's integration or amalgamation into white American society, which is, nevertheless, a definite though little-known fact. Sam Fathers is a symbol of the past and an old culture. The Indians in Faulkner symbolize an inscrutable, mysterious folk culture completely foreign to the white man. The Black man (whom he thinks he understands) he either relates to, condescends toward, or pointedly ignores when it suits his purpose. He can insult the Black man's Blackness by treating him as if he were invisible. But the red man is beyond his understanding, and not a clear or coherent part of either his myth about race or his myth about religion. The white man's guilt toward the red man overwhelms him and he cannot deal rationally with this guilt. In "Red Leaves," "The Bear," and "Was," Faulkner presents us with the red man as part of the great wilderness, totally a part of nature, having integrity only as long as he keeps himself inviolate, free of slavery and miscegenation. When the Indian buys slaves and mixes with white women (for example, as Sam Fathers is the result of the relationship between his mother, a Black slave and his father, a Chickasaw chief), then the Indian's sin is the same as the white man's. He grows weaker and dies or becomes extinct. But this is not really the reason for the extinction of the red man, as we very well know. The red man lost the military battle and war with the white man, but disease was really the white man's tool used to destroy the red man. It was the red man who was massacred into extinction. He is ambivalent and outside the white man's moral code. Faulkner extols the idea of racial purity or integrity regardless of the particular color: red, white, and Black.

Sam Fathers is the pathetic, tragically mixed man, red and Black, yet he seems not to be disturbed either by pathos or tragedy. "The Bear" is therefore the best example of Faulkner's fiction in which the symbolic significance of his three races—red, white, and Black—is carefully interwoven so that theme, action, character, and style are all of one piece. Many teachers and authorities agree that the shorter piece and original "Bear" is a better short story—technically speaking. But in the longer piece the racial ideas, myths, and themes can be seen as giving rise to morality, honor, comments on time, and in general expressing Faulkner's Weltanschauung philosophy and world view.

In Faulkner's world, the "system" that he consciously creates, the worlds of the Old and New Testaments are melded into a myth that accommodates the American myth about race and sees man in an almost fatalistic sense. His fatalism is only ameliorated by his faith in man's spirit—man's heart—man's living soul, a humanism that he says will, in the end, against all odds, prevail.

The student of southern literature must constantly be confronted with the problem of race; race has been an issue throughout the evolution of southern literature and history. Most of us have studied this literature and history as we have observed and been part of the culture. Because of the nature of more than three hundred years of southern history, the student of American literature tends to think only in terms of the achievements of one race; and because of the nature of the two institutions of slavery and segregation, the issue of racism in the literature has only recently been considered. The history and literature of the region are a reflection of the life and culture of the people. Therefore, we encounter racial characters, themes, philosophy, and the southern scene in all of southern literature. But Faulkner represents the first real breakthrough in American literature on the treatment of race, both in terms of philosophy and in terms of technique. Polarity in Faulkner means the juxtaposition of race against race, class against class, reality against imagination, symbolism against realism. In Faulkner we see for the first time the southern white writer rising above time and place, struggling beyond the racist limitations of his society into the truly rarified world of the artist, a world in which human values and universal truths take precedence over the provincial and philistine notions of bigoted minds. Like all great writers, he moves from the local to the universal, from the immediate to the timeless, and from the simple into the sublime. It is toward this idealistic goal that we must all strive. If we cannot dream with the great mythic imagination of Faulkner we can at least aspire toward the splendid failure of his dream.

Acknowledgments

We gratefully acknowledge permission to reprint the following material:

Margaret Walker Alexander: "For My People," "Southern Song," "Sorrow Home," from *For My People* by Margaret Walker, copyright 1942 by Yale University Press. "Giants of My Century," "Five Black Men," from *This Is My Century: New and Collected Poems* by Margaret Walker, copyright 1989 University of Georgia Press. All reprinted by permission of author.

Gwendolyn Brooks: "Gay Chaps at the Bar," "the birth in a narrow room," "The Anniad," from *The World of Gwendolyn Brooks* by Gwendolyn Brooks. Copyright 1971 by Gwendolyn Brooks Blakely. Reprinted by permission of author.

Sterling Brown: "Old Lem," from *The Complete Poems of Sterling Brown* edited by Michael S. Harper, Harper and Row, 1980. Reprinted by permission of publisher and Michael Harper.

Frank Marshall Davis: "Portrait of the Cotton South," from *47th Street* by Frank Marshall Davis. Copyright 1948 Frank Marshall Davis. Reprinted by permission of Beth Charlton, executor of the author's estate.

Owen Dodson: "Conversation on V," from *Powerful Long Ladder* by Owen Dodson. Copyright 1946 by Owen Dodson. Reprinted by permission of Farrar, Straus and Giroux, Inc.

Paul Laurence Dunbar: "Sympathy," from *The Complete Poems of Paul Laurence Dunbar* by Paul Laurence Dunbar. Copyright 1913 by Dodd, Mead and Company. Reprinted by permission of publisher.

Robert Hayden: "Eine Kleine Nachtmusik," from *The Lion and the Archer* by Robert Hayden and Myron O' Higgins. Copyright 1949 by Hemphill Press. Reprinted by permission of publisher.

Myron O' Higgins: "Two Lean Cats," from *The Lion and the Archer* by Robert Hayden and Myron O' Higgins. Copyright 1949 by Hemphill Press. Reprinted by permission of publisher.

Langston Hughes: "Harlem Night Song," from *Selected Poems* by Langston Hughes. Copyright 1926 by Alfred A. Knopf, Inc. Reprinted by permission of the publisher. "Minstrel Man" from *The Dream Keeper and Other Poems* by Langston Hughes. Copyright 1932 by Alfred A. Knopf, Inc. Renewed 1960 by Langston Hughes. Reprinted by peermission of the publisher.

Helene Johnson: "Bottled" from *The Poetry of Black America*, edited by Arnold Adoff, Harper and Row, 1973. Reprinted by permission of publisher.

LeRoi Jones: "Preface to a Twenty Volume Suicide Note," from *Preface to a Twenty Volume Suicide Note* by LeRoi Jones. Copyright 1961 by LeRoi Jones. Reprinted by permission of author.

Don L. Lee: "A Message All Blackpeople Can Dig," from *Don't Cry, Scream* by Don L. Lee. Copyright 1970 by Don L. Lee. Reprinted by permission of author.

Claude McKay: "If We Must Die," from *Selected Poems of Claude McKay* by Claude McKay. Copyright 1936 by Harcourt, Brace and World. Reprinted by permission of Twayne Publishers, G.K. Hall and Co.

Anne Spencer: "Dunbar" from *The Book of Negro Poetry*, edited by James

Printed in the USA
CPSIA information can be obtained
at www.ICGtesting.com
LVHW091515080824
787695LV00001B/128

9 781558 610040